MW00775313

WALKING
with
JESUS

WALKING
with
JESUS

Devotions for Autumn & Thanksgiving 2024

Editors of *Mornings with Jesus*

A GUIDEPOSTS DEVOTIONAL

Walking with Jesus: Devotions for Autumn and Thanksgiving 2024

Published by Guideposts, 100 Reserve Road, Suite E200, Danbury, CT 06810
Guideposts.org

Copyright © 2024 by Guideposts. All rights reserved.

This book, or parts thereof, may not be reproduced, stored in a retrieval system, or transmitted in any form or by any means, electronic, mechanical, photocopying, recording or otherwise, without the written permission of the publisher.

ACKNOWLEDGMENTS

Every attempt has been made to credit the sources of copyrighted material used in this book. If any such acknowledgment has been inadvertently omitted or miscredited, receipt of such information would be appreciated.

Scripture quotations marked (AMPC) are taken from the *Amplified Bible, Classic Edition*. Copyright © 1954, 1958, 1962, 1964, 1965, 1987 by The Lockman Foundation.

Scripture quotations marked (CEB) are taken from the *Common English Bible*. Copyright © 2011 by Common English Bible.

Scripture quotations marked (ESV) are taken from *The Holy Bible, English Standard Version*. Copyright © 2001 by Crossway Bibles, a division of Good News Publishers. Used by permission. All rights reserved.

Scripture quotations marked (HCSB) are taken from the *Holman Christian Standard Bible*. Copyright © 1999, 2000, 2002, 2003, 2009 by Holman Bible Publishers, Nashville, Tennessee. All rights reserved.

Scripture quotations marked (KJV) are taken from the *King James Version of the Bible*.

Scripture quotations marked (MSG) are taken from *The Message*. Copyright © 1993, 2002, 2018 by Eugene H. Peterson.

Scripture quotations marked (NASB) are taken from the *New American Standard Bible*®, Copyright © 1960, 1971, 1977, 1995, 2020 by The Lockman Foundation. All rights reserved.

Scripture quotations marked (NIV) are taken from *The Holy Bible, New International Version*®, *NIV*®. Copyright © 1973, 1978, 1984, 2011 by Biblica, Inc. Used by permission. All rights reserved worldwide.

Scripture quotations marked (NLT) are taken from the *Holy Bible, New Living Translation*. Copyright © 1996, 2004, 2007, 2015 by Tyndale House Foundation. Used by permission of Tyndale House Publishers Inc., Carol Stream, Illinois. All rights reserved.

Scripture quotations marked (NRSVUE) are taken from the *New Revised Standard Version, Updated Edition*. Copyright © 2021 by the National Council of Churches of Christ in the United States of America. Used by permission. All rights reserved worldwide.

Scripture quotations marked (TLB) are taken from *The Living Bible*. Copyright © 1971 by Tyndale House Publishers, Inc., Carol Stream, Illinois. All rights reserved.

Cover and interior design by Pamela Walker, W Design Studio
Cover photo by Dreamstime
Typeset by Aptara, Inc.

ISBN 978-1-961126-97-8 (softcover)
ISBN 978-1-961126-98-5 (epub)

Printed and bound in the United States of America
10 9 8 7 6 5 4 3 2 1

"Every day I ask God for grace. Grace is the infinite love and mercy shown to others. It keeps me humble in the awareness of my small place in the world, and it fills me with gratitude that I have been so unaccountably blessed."

—ROBIN ROBERTS

A Gift from Guideposts

Thank you for your purchase! We appreciate your support and want to express our gratitude with a special gift just for you.

Dive into *Spirit Lifters*, a complimentary booklet that will fortify your faith and offer solace during challenging moments. It contains 31 carefully selected verses from scripture that will soothe your soul and uplift your spirit.

Please use the
QR code or go to
guideposts.org/spiritlifters
to download.

There's not a day in all the year
    But holds some hidden pleasure,
And looking back, joys oft appear
    To brim the past's wide measure.
But blessings are like friends, I hold,
    Who love and labor near us.
We ought to raise our notes of praise
    While living hearts can hear us.

Full many a blessing wears the guise
    Of worry or of trouble;
Far-seeing is the soul, and wise,
    Who knows the mask is double.
But he who has the faith and strength
    To thank his God for sorrow
Has found a joy without alloy
    To gladden every morrow.

We ought to make the moments notes
    Of happy, glad Thanksgiving;
The hours and days a silent phrase
    Of music we are living.
And so the theme should swell and grow
    As weeks and months pass o'er us,
And rise sublime at this good time,
    A grand Thanksgiving chorus.

Excerpted from "Thanksgiving," by Ella Wheeler Wilcox

INTRODUCTION

I will praise God's name in song and glorify him with thanksgiving.

—Psalm 69:30 (NIV)

Like a kaleidoscope, our spiritual perspective shifts with the changing season. Winter ushers in the joy of our Savior's birth and a wealth of holiday cheer. Spring is a season of renewal following months of dormancy, the solemnity of Lent, and the miracle of the Resurrection. And summer's long days are a heavenly banquet for the senses. Fall has traditionally represented harvest—a time not only to gather the bounty of the fields but to pause and recognize the myriad blessings God has lovingly bestowed on us.

As the world around us yields to colder temperatures, the trees trading their greenery for brilliant yellows, oranges, and reds, autumn is a perfect opportunity to appreciate the abundance in our life and enjoy the cozy companionship of the people we hold most dear. How fitting, then, that we celebrate such a beautiful day as Thanksgiving during the fall. As Norman Vincent Peale noted, "If we develop the ability to appreciate, we also develop our capacity to be thankful."

God gives us so many things. In expressing our thanks to Him, we follow on a path that the Bible lays out for us. The New Testament details multiple occasions when Jesus thanks His Father for the resources at His disposal. The Apostle Matthew gives us an especially resonant example: the feast of the loaves and fish. Declining His disciples' request, Jesus refuses to send away the crowds that have gathered to see Him. Instead, He and the disciples will share their own humble provisions. Before the meal can begin, Jesus pauses to offer His gratitude for what they do have:

Taking the five loaves and the two fish and looking up to heaven, he gave thanks and broke the loaves. Then he gave them to the disciples, and the disciples gave them to the people.

—Matthew 14:19 (NIV)

The Gospel tells us that those meager supplies would go on to feed several thousand men, women, and children—even yielding "twelve basketfuls of broken pieces that were left over" (Matthew 14:20). More than enough to satisfy everyone there. There is no earthly reason why everyone could have been fed from such small rations, but as Jesus knew, God makes all things possible.

Though the blessings we experience may not be so overtly miraculous, they are constant, life-affirming, and full of the devotion He has for us. You may even find that offering your gratitude to the Redeemer has an unexpected spiritual benefit, inviting peace and positivity into your heart. The Bible tells us that giving thanks to God is connected to our ability to cast off our worries and look hopefully toward the future. As author and Benedictine monk Brother David Steindl-Rast observes, "We notice that joyful people are grateful and suppose that they are grateful for their joy. But the reverse is true: Their joy springs from gratefulness."

What harvest do you bring to God? Will it be a richness of gratitude for the blessings in your life? As the Lord loves us, His children, He also loves listening to our thanks—both for the momentous events and for the smaller, heartfelt moments that have brought us joy.

Do not be anxious about anything, but in every situation, by prayer and petition, with thanksgiving, present your requests to God.

—Philippians 4:6 (NIV)

The devotions in this book, written by the beloved writers of *Mornings with Jesus*, have been carefully chosen for their various perspectives on autumn's themes. You may already be familiar with many of the authors, whose beautiful personal stories have helped draw many readers closer to Christ. Covering October 1 through November 30, the devotions not only celebrate God's bounty but also share insights on this special cycle of His creation.

Autumn offers a beautiful time to reconnect with the Lord who brings us so much. Its unique rhythms of abundance, appreciation, and thanksgiving can enrich our faith and fill our hearts. Over the next two months, may this book help you embrace the season and the opportunity it gives to strengthen your spiritual relationships. We wish you a journey lightened with gratitude and God's grace as you embark on your next season.

And whatever you do, whether in word or deed, do it all in the name of the Lord Jesus, giving thanks to God the Father through him.

—Colossians 3:17 (NIV)

Lisa Guernsey

OCTOBER

TUESDAY
OCTOBER 1

A merry heart maketh a cheerful countenance.

PROVERBS 15:13 (KJV)

OCTOBER HAS ARRIVED, AND DOWN here in northwest Arkansas the leaves are beginning to turn. There's a chill in the morning air, and it's time to put the fall decorations on the front step and by the street lamps.

About this time a few years ago, when Paxton and Calianne were tiny, we picked out a stand-up scarecrow from the grocery store. They're all over the place these days, and for seven dollars it has been a source of fun memories. Actually, the scarecrow isn't an "it" but a "she," and she has acquired an identity of her own.

The kids dubbed her Pumpkin Girl, and she's as cute as her name, even though she doesn't resemble a pumpkin at all. She's a scarecrow. Well, my husband pulled her down from the garage attic a couple of days ago, and I noticed her standing there this morning when I backed out to do the school run. Something about her smile has stayed with me. Who knew you could learn something about life from a raggedy scarecrow?

What I can't get out of my head is her unflagging look of peace and contentment. Granted, she's an inanimate object, but hear me out. She has weathered winds and rain, even some fierce storms over the years. She has been stuck where we put her, and her outsides show the wear and tear.

But her countenance has not faded. Her smile still lights the doorway to our home. I know that she cannot choose those characteristics, nor does she possess the life to care.

However, I can and I do. Am I choosing to wear Christ's joy on my face despite life's weather? Do I possess enough of Christ's life in me to care?

Long live Pumpkin Girl, and may my countenance light the doorway to Jesus.

ERIN KEELEY MARSHALL

FAITH STEP

Memorize Psalm 89:15 (NLT): "Happy are those who hear the joyful call to worship, for they will walk in the light of your presence, Lord."

WEDNESDAY
OCTOBER 2

Enter his gates with thanksgiving, and his courts
with praise! Give thanks to him; bless his name!

PSALM 100:4 (ESV)

I'VE READ SEVERAL ARTICLES ABOUT the benefits of thank-fulness. Studies show that cultivating feelings of gratitude leads to improved mental and physical health. Increased optimism helps us handle stress better, which in turn boosts our immune system. These studies always remind me that the Bible urges us to make a deliberate choice to have a grateful spirit.

Jesus exposed our human tendency toward a lack of grati-tude in Luke 17. Ten lepers begged Him to heal them. Jesus told them to go to the priests; as they walked, they were healed. Only one man returned to thank Jesus. When I read Jesus's question, "Where are the nine?" I can't help wonder-ing: Do I remember to thank Him for my blessings only one time out of ten?

I decided to be more intentional about developing the right attitude. I bought a journal to write down things for which I'm thankful. At first, I wondered if it might be hard to think of something to record every evening. But God helped me kick-start this habit the very first day. That morning I had prayed that I would hear from my children over the weekend. It had been a while since I'd talked with my sons; they hadn't returned my latest phone calls. Early in the evening, both of them phoned while I was talking with my daughter. I was able to merge the calls and talk to all three of my children at the same time.

Whenever I hesitate to write in my journal at bedtime, all I have to do is read that first entry. Then I think of all kinds of reasons to be grateful.

DIANNE NEAL MATTHEWS

FAITH STEP

Why not develop the habit of beginning or ending your day with gratitude for your blessings? List as many specific reasons to thank Jesus as you can think of.

THURSDAY
OCTOBER 3

[Jesus said,] "The seed scattered on good soil are those who hear the word and embrace it."

MARK 4:20 (CEB)

I N AUTUMN, WHEN THE SUN is warm and everything growing takes on a new look—trees, gardens, lawns—our grandchildren love to skirt the edge of our pond looking for mature cattail pods and milkweed pods.

Say what you will about how both milkweeds and cattails have the potential for becoming a nuisance; they do serve a purpose and provide entertainment for adventurous children.

Our grandkids live near enough that they can observe the entire life cycle of cattails and milkweeds. They appreciate when the cattails' velvety dark brown seedpod matures and when the milkweed seedpods grow plump and start to dry out. In the fall, the children pop open the cattail pods to reveal thousands of white fluff-seeds that silently explode out of the pod. The same for the milkweeds. Breaking open a mature milkweed seedpod sends hundreds or thousands of downy, almost weightless, wispy seeds into the air.

When small hands on our property break open the seedpods, the fluff inside is carried on a breath of a breeze farther than the children imagined possible.

Sometimes we imagine that sharing the truth about Jesus—the Gospel—is far more complicated than it really is. Rather than a dissertation, it's more like breaking open a pod and setting the seeds loose with a puff of our breath.

We open God's Word, expose the hope Jesus brings, and breathe on it with our own story of His Impact on our life and future. The seeds are carried on that breeze...farther than we ever dreamed.

CYNTHIA RUCHTI

FAITH STEP

Take note today of the small things you can do to help spread the good news of Jesus to contribute to a soul's rest. Consider keeping a record of milkweed moments.

FRIDAY
OCTOBER 4

Think about the things of heaven, not the things of earth. For you died to this life, and your real life is hidden with Christ in God.

COLOSSIANS 3:2–3 (NLT)

PREPARING TO MOVE ABOARD A sailboat meant purging nearly all our earthly belongings. The only other option was to rent a storage unit nearby, but that seemed like unwise stewardship. "It's cheaper to replace those belongings when we return to shore than to pay storage fees for several years," Gene assured me.

I sorted through closets, cupboards, and drawers. I donated and sold clothing, appliances, books, home décor, and furniture. Parting with my possessions came more easily than I'd expected with the exception of two items—our mattress and my favorite leather love seat.

The mattress was less than three years old and one of the best purchases we'd ever made. Its firmness helped me sleep well every night. The love seat was my sacred space—it's where I enjoyed my quiet time with Jesus, wrote my devotional blogs, and cuddled my grandbabies. It represented my "home sweet home" after each overseas ministry trip.

The anticipation of parting with these items pained me until Jesus whispered, *Am I not enough for you?* His words, gently spoken, challenged my perspective. He'd given His life for my sake. Could I not give up a mattress and love seat for Him? Sure, these things had brought me deep satisfaction, but would I not experience even greater satisfaction in knowing my obedience brought Jesus pleasure?

"Yes, Jesus. You are enough," I whispered. "Thank you for loaning me these gifts and for the joy they've brought. Now I give them back to you."

GRACE FOX

FAITH STEP

Look around your home. What possessions bring you joy? Consider giving away one of these beloved items as an act of worship or a demonstration of your willingness to share with others the blessings Jesus has given you.

SATURDAY
OCTOBER 5

But, as it is written, "What no eye has seen, nor ear heard, nor the heart of man imagined, what God has prepared for those who love him."

1 CORINTHIANS 2:9 (ESV)

IN THE WEEKS BEFORE MY husband's autumn birthday, he mentioned that fall would be a good time to find a grill on sale at one of the local hardware stores. Thinking it would be a great birthday surprise, my daughter headed to the store and texted me pictures of various options. Together we decided on a big shiny model, which the store put in the back of the van for her.

Once she got it home, the two of us looked like a Laurel and Hardy movie as we muscled the heavy box onto a dolly, wobbled it down a hill at the side of the house, and squeezed it through the back door. Next we pulled bins and furniture out of the back basement room we use for storage, and worked to hide a box the size of a small house.

In the following weeks, we hoped my husband wouldn't start a project that necessitated digging for something in the storage room. There would be no way to hide the surprise if he looked too closely.

The night before his birthday, I signaled my daughter once my husband was asleep, and she hauled the box out and assembled the grill. The next morning I led him downstairs, and all of our efforts were rewarded when we heard his laughter at the sight of the huge grill assembled in the family room. Surprising him was a delight.

I hear a similar delight in Jesus's words throughout the Gospels. He is preparing something wonderful for each of us in the next life. We get hints in Scripture, but much is a surprise. But we can trust that the surprises are prepared with love and will bring us great joy.

SHARON HINCK

FAITH STEP

Plan a small surprise for someone you love. Think about how Jesus is planning good things for you, as well.

SUNDAY
OCTOBER 6

Therefore, if anyone is in Christ, he is a
new creation; old things have passed away,
and look, new things have come.

2 CORINTHIANS 5:17 (HCSB)

M Y SON PIERCE'S FIRST BASKETBALL season after we
moved to Florida was wonderful. The coach was a
longtime resident and former local star, a seasoned pro who
skillfully affirmed the kids, bringing out their best. He and
Pierce built a nice rapport, and we looked forward to having
the same coach next season.

But when the draft came around, Pierce was picked by
another coach, who was just plain different than his beloved
first coach. Seeing Pierce's disappointment, I tried hard to
conceal my own, urging him to keep an open mind and
reminding him that he'd have a lot of different coaches over
time. Still, Pierce was sad and anxious about the change.

As the season went on, I made a point to avoid the sub-
ject, not wanting to pick a scab. Finally, a few weeks into

the season, I asked Pierce how the new coach was working out.

"Oh, he is so great," he said with sincere enthusiasm. "He's just really nice and has taught me so much." He went on and on about his new coach's outstanding qualities and impact. Indeed, the team gelled and made it to the championship game, losing only by a few points to the reigning champions. As awesome as his former coach was, Pierce's new coach was an even better fit.

Kids deliver so many lessons! How often have I dreaded a "last season" loss and dreaded the "new season" only to find the new season was better than ever? Can I trust that Jesus knows best with matters of greater importance? Yes!

ISABELLA CAMPOLATTARO

FAITH STEP

Are you facing a disappointing change to the unfamiliar and unexpected? Thank God for last season and trust God with your new season. In Christ, the new has come!

MONDAY
OCTOBER 7

For of His fullness we have all received,
and grace upon grace.

JOHN 1:16 (NASB)

I HAVE A STUDENT IN freshman English who is 60 years old. He told me he joined the army to get the GI Bill, so he could go to college over 40 years ago. Instead, he went to Vietnam. When he came home, he said, he was too messed up to start college. He's had a difficult life but never gave up his dream.

For years, he's been haunted by nightmares that drove him to alcohol addiction. His family left him alone on his farm. Finally he got help and learned he has PTSD. Guess what the cure is? Get out of isolation. So now, using his GI Bill, he's in my class.

This guy could focus on everything that's sad about his story. Just listening to it brought me to tears. But instead, he chooses to focus on the new life he's finding after all these years. He brings an enthusiasm to class that encourages me.

An attitude of gratitude, as the saying goes. What a difference it makes when one approaches life through the lens of grace.

It's by grace, he believes, that he's alive. By grace his family left him because it forced him to get help. He found grace in the VA (Veterans Administration). It's by grace that he found out he has PTSD. And grace that he can do something to help dispel the darkness in his mind.

This story has helped me to remember that grace is everywhere. There's grace for us in everything. And the source of grace is Jesus. Out of His fullness, grace flows freely and abundantly forever.

GWEN FORD FAULKENBERRY

FAITH STEP

Pour out a cup of sugar and try to count the individual granules. The number you get? Not even close to how much grace is yours in Jesus.

TUESDAY
OCTOBER 8

*Put on your new nature, and be renewed as you
learn to know your Creator and become like him.*

COLOSSIANS 3:10 (NLT)

WE STARTED A GARDEN THIS past spring, and planted
fruit and nut trees and began to compost. Admittedly, we aren't always in tune with moderation; it was a lot
of work, but we're excited about the blessings these ventures
hold for our family's health.

To create compost for the garden, we bought a worm
factory. It's a multilevel bin that came with one thousand
worms that have procreated into scads more. We feed them
produce, bread, and other goodies.

Last week my husband checked on the worms and saw
small potatoes growing in the bin. We hadn't put any into
it, just some potato peels. But right before his eyes, potatoes
had sprouted and found new life.

Next, he went out to the garden and dug in the dirt where
he had removed our dead potato plants a few weeks earlier.

He had already removed all the potatoes, but sure enough he found three more new ones. So I cooked them up, and we ate them with supper.

Who knew fresh growth could come from what had aged and gone bad?

This object lesson speaks to me most clearly on days when the fruit of my spirit doesn't exactly measure up to the quality of the Fruit of Jesus's Spirit. I love that today's verse says that, as we know our Savior better, our nature continues to be renewed. If we are His, then we have this ever fresh source of life growing within us.

So when I'm feeling less than gracious, when mercy isn't thriving in my life, and when I'm tempted to cast off the power of gentleness, I can take a deep breath and thank Jesus that He is ready to renew me again. Only then can I be a consistent refreshment to others.

ERIN KEELEY MARSHALL

FAITH STEP

Read Colossians 3:12–14 to find out the qualities of this new nature.

WEDNESDAY
OCTOBER 9

*"Follow God's example, therefore, as dearly loved
children and walk in the way of love, just
as Christ loved us and gave himself up for us
as a fragrant offering and sacrifice to God."*

EPHESIANS 5:1–2 (NIV)

MY HUSBAND AND I ARE both tea drinkers. I fuel my
writing work with pot after pot of Irish Breakfast or
English Teatime with some Darjeeling or Good Earth to
keep things interesting. Ted chases down supper with a big
mug of iced tea. Plain old Lipton is his preference, and we
brew up a pitcher every day or two to keep in the fridge.

In the morning, when I'm blinking owlishly, trying to
figure out what day it is, Ted brews a pot of morning tea and
brings a mug of steamy heaven to me. And when I notice
the pitcher in the fridge is close to empty, I brew another
batch of iced tea for him.

Now logic would say that it would be just as easy for Ted
to brew the iced tea for himself, and for me to make the

hot tea for myself. Both tasks take about the same amount of time.

But by doing it for each other, the tea means more. It becomes a gift of love.

Thinking about that phenomenon made me wonder about other places in my life where I could apply that concept. Living in Christian community means sometimes doing something for others even when they could do it for themselves. Community also means accepting gifts of love even when I could have managed on my own. It's interdependence. It's a choice to look out for the needs of another.

SHARON HINCK

FAITH STEP

Can you think of someone in your life who could use some Orange Pekoe with a little lemon and sugar? Maybe they don't look like they need it, but offer it anyway. Our small acts of love can make a huge difference to the people around us.

THURSDAY
OCTOBER 10

Be patient until the Lord's coming. See how the farmer waits for the precious fruit of the earth and is patient with it until it receives the early and the late rains. You also must be patient. Strengthen your hearts, because the Lord's coming is near.

JAMES 5:7–8 (HCSB)

SINCE I GREW UP AS a farmer's daughter, I can easily relate to agricultural illustrations in the Bible. I remember my dad watching the weather, hoping our dusty cotton fields would get enough rain to keep the plants healthy and lead to a good harvest. Those few cotton bales represented our main source of income—some years, the only source. My dad sowed the crops in spring; we had to wait until after we chopped weeds all summer and then picked the cotton in autumn to see if the money would be enough to cover us for a year.

Waiting is just plain hard, but Jesus calls us to exercise spiritual patience. That's the kind we need as we go through life's daily temptations, disappointments, and troubles that shake us to the core. As we struggle to think and respond in a godly way. As we watch the news and feel like the world has gone mad. As we wait year after year for answers to the prayer that represents our deepest longing.

A farmer doesn't know for sure that the rains will come; drought is always a possibility. But thanks to God's Word, we can know some things with certainty. Our trials and sufferings—and waiting—will produce a harvest of righteousness in our hearts and lives. And one day, Jesus will return to the earth to eradicate evil and put things right. These promises are what help us persevere, no matter what field we work in.

DIANNE NEAL MATTHEWS

FAITH STEP

What are you waiting for today? Ask Jesus to strengthen your heart and help you wait patiently, trusting that the harvest will come.

FRIDAY
OCTOBER 11

"They all gave out of their wealth; but she, out of her poverty, put in everything—all she had to live on."

MARK 12:44 (NIV)

IN THE MID-1990S, OUR FAMILY lived in an Atlanta suburb with homes nicer than any we'd lived in previously. However, in the high-profile Georgia capital, we merely blended with the upper-middle-class. Everyone had money. Everyone spent money. It was the world before any economic struggles.

During this time, our family met a single mother named Elizabeth at our second visit to church. Not only did she welcome us, but she wasted no time asking us to join her family for lunch after a service.

Two Sundays later, we followed Elizabeth to an older home a few miles away. Then she and her three children led us around to the basement entrance. This was their home. A picnic table defined their dining area, and their bedrooms were closet-size sections off of the main room.

During the time we spent with her family, we enjoyed a delicious meal and amazing spiritual fellowship. Her family was gracious and happy, filled with God's spirit, in spite of their meager surroundings.

We found ourselves mentioning the uplifting visit throughout the week and ashamed that, in spite of all we had, we hadn't been content. We began wanting to give more, do more—be more like Elizabeth.

The next Sunday I mentioned our wonderful lunch to another couple. They explained that every family at the church had received a welcoming meal from this single mom. Our church had over 1,600 members, and she'd fed each and every one.

RENEE ANDREWS

FAITH STEP

Today follow Elizabeth's example. If you are struggling and feel you have nothing to offer, you can share a meal or a smile. If you live in abundance, give abundantly. But no matter what you have, give like the widow.

SATURDAY
OCTOBER 12

*Come to me, all you who are weary and
burdened, and I will give you rest.*

MATTHEW 11:28 (NIV)

A LONG WITH BEING STILL, rest is a theme Jesus has brought to my attention this past year. (Have you found Jesus is always seeking to teach you something?) The way Jesus's loving intent has come to light is the intersection of my desperate need for rest and a bevy of messengers repeatedly urging me to "rest."

Stillness and rest, I'm finding, are not the same thing but are close cousins. In my case, the call to stillness came first. I had to carve out time to be still to hear and fully understand the invitation to rest.

In my case, rest is not about spending more time relaxing or having fun. It's a state of mind that informs my very being. Rest means that no matter what's going on, I'm trusting Jesus is ordering my steps, solving my problems, providing, refining me—lovingly, completely, and right on time. It mostly feels like going with the flow, enjoying my life.

Yet neither stillness nor rest is passive. They both depend entirely on the intimacy of my relationship with Jesus—a level of intimacy that, as with any relationship, comes only with time, nearness, and attention to Him.

This idea of rest is gradually revolutionizing my life as I lean into it more and more. *Could it have always been this simple? Could I have skipped some of my striving and anxious analyzing and gone straight to rest?* I don't know. Maybe everything has led me here, right on time.

ISABELLA CAMPOLATTARO

FAITH STEP

Consider Christ's invitation to rest in Him. Seek to learn how you can receive Jesus's rest in your current situation.

SUNDAY
OCTOBER 13

*For everything there is a season, a time for every
activity under heaven. A time to be born and a
time to die. A time to plant and a time to harvest.
A time to kill and a time to heal. A time to tear
down and a time to build up. A time to cry and a
time to laugh. A time to grieve and a time to dance.*

ECCLESIASTES 3:1–4 (NLT)

THIS IS ADDISON'S LAST YEAR in elementary school. There
are no superheroes on his backpack. It's all black with
gray trim. Because life is serious now. He has started slicking
his hair over to one side. He looks like a young executive
heading off to class. There are no lingering drop-offs or
goodbye kisses at school. It is all about quick waves and
head nods now.

It is amazing how quickly the seasons of life fly past. It
seems like moments ago that Addie was a baby riding on my
hip. And now? I would throw out my hip if I tried to pick
him up. Sometimes I get a little teary when I think about

how fast time goes. But I don't want to get stuck reminiscing about the past. I want to soak up this season of Addison growing and changing and slicking back his hair.

Jesus has given each season of our lives its own joys and struggles. He doesn't want us clinging to seasons past, longing for the way things used to be. He has grace and peace for the moment we are living right now. He has new hopes and truth for this day and this day alone. We don't want to miss out on today's beauty. We need to soak it up. Revel in it. Sing and dance. And embrace the season we are living out with gratitude.

SUSANNA FOTH AUGHTMON

FAITH STEP

What are you thankful for in this season of your life? Put a Gratitude List on your fridge as a daily reminder of Jesus's goodness.

MONDAY
OCTOBER 14

No man can serve two masters: for either
he will hate the one, and love the other; or else
he will hold to the one, and despise the other.
Ye cannot serve God and mammon.

MATTHEW 6:24 (KJV)

RIGHT NOW I'M WATCHING WHITECAPS crash against the shore while rain streaks the windows facing Lake Superior. I'm snug and warm, holding a mug of tea, savoring the rhythms of nature. Our friends own this cabin, and they invited my husband and me to use it. Everywhere I turn there are cozy details, beauty, and comforts. Yet they wrote in their guest book that they consider themselves simply stewards of this beautiful home that God provided for them.

Their example inspired me to think about stewardship. How does Jesus want us to view the belongings that have come under our care?

In Matthew 6, the word translated as *mammon* is most likely derived from the Aramaic term for "the treasure a person trusts in." Modern translations use the word *money*, but the original meaning helps me apply Jesus's words more widely. When we look around our home, some possessions were earned by hard work and some items were gifts. However they came to us, Jesus reminds us that if we put our trust in these things, they can become our masters and steal away our service to Him.

That's why the concept of stewardship is so helpful. We can view any item and ask, "How can I use this to serve Jesus?" Our mixer can be used to bake a cake for a sick friend. Our books can be lent to a classmate searching for truth. We could even lend our home—as our friends did—to a couple needing a quiet place to be refreshed.

SHARON HINCK

FAITH STEP

Walk through your home with new eyes, as a steward rather than an owner. Ask Jesus to show you ways you can serve Him with the array of items under your roof.

TUESDAY
OCTOBER 15

This is the confidence that we have toward him,
that if we ask anything according to his will he
hears us. And if we know that he hears us in
whatever we ask, we know that we have
the requests that we have asked of him.

1 JOHN 5:14–15 (ESV)

FOR YEARS I WANTED TO plant a plethora of tulips in my yard, but other priorities kept taking over. And then finally I took the plunge, and fifty-some tulip bulbs went in the ground—a solid start. Now I just need to wait out the winter for the fruits of my labors to push up from the earth to show off their radiance. Sure, some may not turn out as I'd anticipated, but I can believe that planting them triggered a response in each bulb.

Over these next months, I have several prayer requests I'm planning to commit to Jesus. Just like those tulips are designed to respond to being planted, when I plant my prayers with Jesus, I can trust that He will deliver an answer.

His answer may sometimes be no, and sometimes it may be wait, and sometimes it may be a different color or variety than I expected.

Planting prayers always yields a response from Jesus because of His promise in 1 John 5:14–15. I pray to connect with Him first of all, and even when I don't see the answer for a long time—sometimes not in this lifetime—I can still trust that every prayer triggers a response from the heavenly throne room where Jesus sits at God's right hand.

Plant a prayer today and trust that each one will yield a response from Jesus…every time.

ERIN KEELEY MARSHALL

FAITH STEP

Buy a packet of bulbs or seeds and watch them grow, letting your faith grow too, knowing Jesus hears and acts on your behalf, even when all seems quiet.

WEDNESDAY
OCTOBER 16

*Every good and perfect gift is from above, coming
down from the Father of the heavenly lights,
who does not change like shifting shadows.*

JAMES 1:17 (NIV)

WHEN A WRITERS' CONFERENCE SPEAKER encouraged us
to start a Blessings Folder, I knew it would be a good
idea. My life was falling apart, making it difficult to see anything positive. The speaker passed out copies of her favorite
Bible verse and a funny story to get us started. As soon as I
got home, I put them in a folder, along with a story that my
oldest son had published. My Blessings Folder became one of
my lifelines during a dark time, as I filled it with encouraging
cards that arrived right when I needed them, notes about
miraculous provisions, and other mementos. Every treasure
that I added to the folder felt like a present from Jesus, saying, *I'm still here, and you still have a lot of good in your life.*

One day, I discovered that I'd run out of room in my folder.
I moved my collection to a pretty box. My Blessings Box now

sits on a shelf in my closest, stuffed beyond capacity—a sweet reminder of the many gifts that came from Jesus at a time when it seemed like life would never be good again.

"Every good and perfect gift is from above...." We don't need to be overwhelmed or grieving to have a reason to collect blessings. In fact, it is often when everything is going well that we miss out on them. When we make a practice of paying attention to how Jesus takes care of us and shows us *I am with you; I know what you need; I know what will make you smile*, we gain the ability to see the littlest things as gifts.

JEANETTE HANSCOME

FAITH STEP

Start a Blessings Box or put a few items in the one you have that felt like gifts from Jesus when you received them.

THURSDAY
OCTOBER 17

*For whosoever shall do the will of my
Father which is in heaven, the same is
my brother, and sister, and mother.*

MATTHEW 12:50 (KJV)

M Y MATERNAL FAMILY CELEBRATES MOST holidays in
my mother's cozy home. When we gather there, her
crowded kitchen bustles with twenty guests or more. They
go back and forth, passing plates and clinking serving dishes
as everyone engages in lively chatter or family stories that
never grow old.

Throughout my mother's home, there are happy faces
in the crowd who are not kinfolk. Georgie, Carol, Verna,
David, and Maxine attend my mother's church. By the
world's standards, they are merely our "good friends."

These five friends have gathered in my mother's home for
more than 30 years. Their faces are featured prominently
in our family photographs. We enjoy their company completely. They vacation with our family and attend our family

reunion. They attend our family birthday parties, school graduations, weddings, and funerals. When they are sick, we, like a loving family, come to their aid. When we are sick, they, like a loving family, come to our aid. While they are not blood relatives, we are deeply connected. Our friends love the Lord, and it is the blood of Jesus that makes us kin.

Jesus said in Matthew 12:50 that His family was anybody who lived to do the will of God.

These encouraging words help us know that wherever we travel or reside, we are not alone. As with Jesus, who found companionship with Mary, Martha, and Lazarus, it is possible for us to share a family connection with friends who live to serve the Lord.

ALICE THOMPSON

FAITH STEP

This morning, pray for the friends who are like family.

FRIDAY
OCTOBER 18

Surely the lowborn are but a breath, the
highborn are but a lie. If weighed on a balance,
they are nothing; together they are only a breath.
Do not trust in extortion or put vain hope in
stolen goods; though your riches increase,
do not set your heart on them.

PSALM 62:9–10 (NIV)

I RECENTLY READ THE STORY about a husband and wife who
had a rocky marriage. They took the extreme measure
of moving to a foreign country to try to salvage their relationship. They had to simplify to enormous measures—no
car, no television, no high-paying jobs. Without all the
distractions of their "stuff," they found their hearts and souls
healing. They grew closer to God and closer to each other.

Jesus warns about riches in numerous places in the
Gospels, and sometimes it's easy to gloss over the words, to
let the meanings slip in one ear and out the other. After all,
most of us aren't *rich*. We're "comfortable" or "content." Yet

we have closets of clothes, spare rooms with boxes, garages full of stuff.

I'm not saying to sell everything you have and give the money to the poor, nor do you have to go live in a foreign country. But if you simplified your life—if you got rid of more stuff than you're comfortable giving away—would you be able to hear Jesus better without the physical, emotional, and spiritual clutter? After all, this world is passing away, and our bodies with it. Can we simplify, getting rid of our things and trusting Jesus for our memories, for the lessons learned, for the needs we have?

CAMY TANG

FAITH STEP

Take a moment to really pray and see if you're holding on to things or to riches that are distracting you from Him. Pray for help to get rid of it. Be willing no matter how drastic it might be, because Jesus will be more than enough for all your needs.

SATURDAY
OCTOBER 19

"Let anyone who is thirsty come to me and drink. Whoever believes in me, as Scripture has said, rivers of living water will flow from within them."

JOHN 7:37–38 (NIV)

I LOVE BEING NEAR WATER. Whether I'm at the coast, a creek, or a lakeside, it settles me. But my favorite place is along the banks of the river running through my town. The Willamette is wide, with beautiful old trees and countless birds calling it home.

As I watch this river, I sense Jesus's peace and power while the massive flow moves past with barely a ripple. Picking up stones to toss in, I feel my transformation as He smooths away my rough edges. When I spot fish struggling upstream, I understand the challenges they face. Jesus teaches me to push forward, to never give up.

Yesterday evening, I walked the bank. The heat of the day was gone, replaced by a coolness hinting at autumn's glory. A gentle breeze carried the welcome scents of dust and falling leaves. As I rounded a bend, sunset lit the water's surface with a soft white glow, resembling molten silver. The image was emblazoned in my mind, depicting the way my soul is being refined.

But the picture I hold close is of the living water that flows within me. Like a stone in that river, I'm following the course He's set for me through my obedience, rejoicing within the freedom of His boundaries. I trust His guidance around every bend, secure in the knowledge He knows the way. I'm willing and ready to guide others I meet along the curves of my life, leading them to Jesus and praying they need never thirst again.

HEIDI GAUL

FAITH STEP

Visit a body of water near you. Listen and watch as Jesus speaks to you in the stillness of a lake, the rush of crashing waves, or the babbling of a brook. Offer a prayer of thanks.

SUNDAY
OCTOBER 20

*Being confident of this, that he who began
a good work in you will carry it on to
completion until the day of Christ Jesus.*

PHILIPPIANS 1:6 (NIV)

YEARS AGO, I FELL IN love with quilting. I watched a
quilting show on television and followed the instruc-
tions to learn different squares and patterns. I started small,
making quilted potholders and Christmas ornaments as
gifts. Then as our tenth wedding anniversary approached,
I decided to surprise my husband with a full-size sampler
quilt, complete with an embroidered wedding verse and our
names and wedding date.

Making several squares, I started out well. A few edges
didn't match up perfectly, and some points in a star or
arrow were a bit blunted. But the colors were beautiful, and
each new pattern was fun to learn. However, my life was
busy with work, school, and children. My quilting supplies
waited in a bin for months at a time. Our tenth anniversary

came and went. Every now and then, I'd pull out the fabric and make one more square.

Years later I pieced together all the squares and completed the backing, filling, and quilting. What I thought would be a short-term project wasn't finished until our seventeenth anniversary.

There are days when I feel like my life is a fabric bin full of half-finished projects. I take comfort in this verse from Philippians. Unlike me, Jesus doesn't abandon His work for months at a time. He works in our lives constantly. He begins a good work and, piece by piece, creates new purpose, new means of service, and conforms us to the pattern He envisions. He never gives up on us.

SHARON HINCK

FAITH STEP

Choose one task that's been waiting for your efforts and work on it today. As you make a little progress, thank Jesus for faithfully bringing His plans for your life to completion.

MONDAY
OCTOBER 21

*"There is more to life than food and
more to the body than clothing."*

LUKE 12:23 (CEB)

A CRISIS AT HOME HELPED put "things" in perspective,
as crises often do. So does the Word of God, but we
humans too often wait for the crisis to remind us what the
Bible already had been saying to our hearts.

We lost a lot of minor things in a fire. The insurance
inventory took several pages to print out, but some were
as small as "lemon pepper, vegetable peeler, spatula, toast
tongs, cereal…"

The remediation team scrubbed and rubbed some of the
decorations I'd had sitting on top of the cupboards. At one
point, I asked them to stop. They were just things. Nothing
precious about them. I'd grown tired of them years ago, but
hadn't the heart to toss them. Now I could. I saw them in a
clearer light. Clutter.

Jesus isn't the typical picture of a homeless man. But He somehow managed to survive three years of ministry—travel included—without owning anything except the clothes on His back, for all we know. He enjoyed good food during feast times, created it at others, fished to feed His friends, appreciated the beauty of the Temple, felt blessed when invited to stay in a nice home. He and His Father were accustomed to providing things for those who needed them.

But He lived and taught that life does not consist in the accumulation of things (Luke 12:23).

It's a lesson that sometimes gets burned into the soul with flames.

I have only one spatula now. It's enough.

But I must say I'm grateful the fire didn't reach the dishwasher.

CYNTHIA RUCHTI

FAITH STEP

Not for the sake of more cupboard space, but as an exercise in perspective, empty a cupboard today. Thank the Lord for what He's given. Donate anything of worth and toss the insignificant. You may be surprised how large a garbage bag you need.

TUESDAY
OCTOBER 22

He poured water into a basin and began
to wash his disciples' feet.

JOHN 13:5 (NIV)

T HE PREACHER AT OUR CHURCH recently taught on the passage in the gospel of John in which Jesus washes the disciples' feet. He described how the scene might have looked as the disciples sat around the table eating that last supper in ancient Jerusalem. One point he made is that their feet were most likely filthy. Crusted with dust and worse from the city streets, they probably even stank.

Jesus's act of washing His disciples' feet was an act of total humility. It was a service usually rendered by a slave, someone designated for grub work, which is not the job description of a King. And yet there He was, going around the room with the cloth and basin of water. The disciples might not have remembered all of the things He taught them, but I bet none of them ever forgot this example of what it means to love.

A similar thing happened in our church. I think many of us would agree that the teaching brought by our pastor was good, and we learned from it. But what's been more extraordinary is the example he set. The next week someone noticed our pastor mulching the flower beds at church. When asked, jokingly, if he was on the Buildings and Grounds Committee now, he answered, "Nope. It was just a great opportunity to wash some feet."

I think the lesson here is at least twofold. The first is that if we want to be like Jesus, we'll lead by example, not only words. And the second is this: loving people means you serve them. Sometimes you have to get your hands dirty.

GWEN FORD FAULKENBERRY

FAITH STEP

Be on the lookout today for dirty feet. You may just get the chance to love by example!

WEDNESDAY
OCTOBER 23

Ever since I first heard of your strong faith in the Lord Jesus and your love for God's people everywhere, I have not stopped thanking God for you. I pray for you constantly.

EPHESIANS 1:15–16 (NLT)

PAUL'S ATTITUDE OF GRATITUDE AMAZES me. Several times throughout his letters in the New Testament he mentioned "remembering" others and giving thanks for them. The book of Ephesians is one of Paul's epistles that records his frequent habit. Having spent two years in Ephesus previously, Paul wrote this book in prison, possibly under house arrest.

Okay, maybe he did have more time to focus and remember in this more isolated setting. But knowing Paul, he still spent time not only writing but also sharing about Jesus to anyone who crossed his path.

Paul didn't thank Jesus once for the beloved friends and new believers he'd met, then forget about them. He "never stopped." Obviously, he had ministered to them. But they also touched his life. And then Paul did more than just remember those people. He prayed constantly for them.

When Jesus spoke to Paul (then Saul) on the road to Damascus and blinded him temporarily, He changed the former persecutor's life—dramatically (Acts 9). That encounter not only resulted in a dynamic missionary preacher but a spirit of gratitude forever in Paul's life.

After reviewing Paul's letter I decided to top my new "thanksgiving" list with the names of people Jesus has brought into my life through the years: friends, family, church members, neighbors—whoever Jesus brings to mind.

Remembering so many may be challenging, and the list will keep growing. But if I can simply ask Jesus to help me maintain a grateful heart, and review that list of names often, that's a good start.

REBECCA BARLOW JORDAN

FAITH STEP

Make a list of people who have influenced your life. Then write notes to let them know how grateful you are, and that you are praying for them.

THURSDAY
OCTOBER 24

I will meditate on your majestic, glorious splendor and your wonderful miracles.

PSALM 145:5 (NLT)

TODAY MY FIVE-YEAR-OLD DAUGHTER ASKED me to come outside to sit with her. I did, and when she sat on my lap on the lawn chair, we laid back our heads and looked at the sky. A cool wind blew on our faces, and we looked at the clouds drifting by. In 15 minutes' time we watched three flocks of birds and saw four airplanes fly overhead.

My plan was to finish folding laundry and cleaning the kitchen. I'm so glad she talked me into her plan. By stepping away from my busywork, and taking time to "look up," I was able to connect with God's creation. I found joy in marveling at clouds, at the flight of birds, and at the wonder of airplanes!

So many times in our lives we forget to look up. We focus on the daily tasks and forget the marvel of Jesus, Who will one day descend in the clouds. We forget to ponder God's amazing design of all creatures. We forget to appreciate how we humans are made in God's image and are able to create and explore. We get so busy with what is seen, that we forget that we are hidden with Christ in God. We forget that this world is only temporary, and what matters most—our life in God—has yet to be revealed.

It takes only 15 minutes of stillness to help you remember…and sometimes a five-year-old to encourage you to stop and look at the sky!

TRICIA GOYER

FAITH STEP

Take 15 minutes today to sit outside, stare at the sky, and marvel at the wonder of God.

FRIDAY
OCTOBER 25

The Word gave life to everything that was
created, and his life brought light to everyone.
The light shines in the darkness, and
the darkness can never extinguish it.

JOHN 1:4–5 (NLT)

LIGHT IS EASY TO TAKE for granted because it shows up every morning without our help and without our consciously thinking about it. Truth is, we need it desperately:

Light enables us to see. Without it, we're cast into pitch-black darkness.

Light sustains plant life. Without it, plants die. That means oxygen disappears. And if oxygen disappears, then other life dies too.

Light sustains earth's temperatures. Remove it, and our planet turns into a celestial ice sphere.

Physical light sustains physical life. The same principle holds true in the spiritual realm, so it's no wonder Jesus made this declaration: "I am the light of the world.

If you follow me, you won't be stumbling through the darkness, because you will have the light that leads to life" (John 8:12).

By calling Himself "the light of the world," Jesus implied that He alone is the source and sustainer of spiritual life. Apart from Him, it cannot exist. In Him we find salvation, and in Him we are fulfilled.

Our society encourages us to look elsewhere for spiritual fulfillment, but everything it suggests is worthless. Even regular church attendance alone isn't enough to give spiritual life and health.

Knowing Jesus and pursuing a vital relationship with Him—the Light of the world—is what gives abundant life now and eternal life tomorrow. We dare not take Him for granted for we need Him desperately.

GRACE FOX

FAITH STEP

Buy a small plant and place it in a sealed paper bag or darkened place in your home for 2 weeks. Note the condition of its leaves when you retrieve it. Compare this to your spiritual life apart from regular time in the Light's presence.

SATURDAY
OCTOBER 26

Love must be sincere. Hate what is evil; cling to what is good. Be devoted to one another in love. Honor one another above yourselves.

ROMANS 12:9–10 (NIV)

FRIDAY AFTERNOONS, FRIENDS GATHER IN my living room for Bible study. We've been a small group for over a decade, working our way through various topics, sharing all the joys and heartaches of life, and praying together. Each woman shares her love for Jesus in different and remarkable kinds of service: family life, careers, mission trips, serving the church through teaching, singing, or administrating.

I treasure our times together. After a week apart, everyone is eager to catch up. We go around the circle, and each person gives updates on her work, family, needs, and answers to prayer.

Recently, I've noticed a problem in my heart. As others share, I begin to grow restless. Instead of listening intently, I silently prioritize the many things about my life that I want to talk about when it's my turn. My selfish heart is so prone to think that my struggles are worse than others' or my updates more exciting. I'd give my life for any of the women in our small group, yet I struggle to be quiet and listen. Laughable, but also pathetic. When Jesus nudged me to look at my attitudes, it was as if He were shining a laser pointer onto my heart. What I saw sent me to my knees, grateful for His forgiveness.

I've always thought that honoring others above myself meant giving up a place in line, or a seat on the bus, or the biggest piece of dessert. I've begun to realize that giving up my selfish mental chatter and truly listening—not jumping in with advice, not interrupting, not impatiently waiting for my turn—is an important way to show love.

SHARON HINCK

FAITH STEP

In your next conversation, honor the other person above yourself and reflect Jesus's love by fully listening.

SUNDAY
OCTOBER 27

Then Peter came to Jesus and asked, "Lord, how many times shall I forgive my brother or sister when he sins against me? Up to seven times?" Jesus answered, "I tell you, not seven times, but seventy-seven times."

MATTHEW 18:21–22 (NIV)

I TRUDGED THROUGH THE AIRPORT LOOKING for the right gate. My back already ached from handling the carry-on bag and the rolling briefcase. *Why did I bring all this stuff?* I inwardly moaned. Since I'd needed to do some work during my visit to my daughter's family, I had packed my heavy laptop and a few reference books. At the last minute, I'd tossed in my day planner.

And of course, I simply had to have all the technology stuff, along with the necessary cords and chargers. My carry-on bag bulged with an extra pair of shoes and clothes I hadn't even worn—not to mention all the lotions and potions I could have done without. I couldn't help casting envious glances at those people who walked by with a single tote bag or backpack slung over their shoulders.

The aches from dealing with heavy luggage are nothing compared to the injuries we cause ourselves by lugging around a different kind of baggage. Jesus wants to help us let go of the heavy burden of past hurts and wrongs that have been done to us. During Jesus's day, Jewish rabbis taught that a person should forgive someone who wronged them, but only three times. Jesus introduced a revolutionary principle: forgiveness without limits.

It's hard to forgive someone who has hurt me; it's also difficult to forgive myself for past mistakes and poor decisions. I can only cultivate a forgiving spirit by depending on Jesus moment by moment to help me make that conscious decision, and by remembering how much He has forgiven me. Jesus knows that if I let go of the burden of unforgivingness, I'll enjoy a lighter spirit, a peaceful mind, more energy and healthier relationships. And I'll know the freedom of packing light for my life's journey.

DIANNE NEAL MATTHEWS

FAITH STEP

Whom do you need to forgive today—yourself
or someone else?

MONDAY
OCTOBER 28

"What then shall we do?"

LUKE 3:10 (ESV)

THE APPLES ON THE TREES lining our south yard were small. Even from a distance, my husband, Bill, and I could see that many on the middle tree were worm-eaten or scar-skinned, unlikely to produce food for those of us who care about fresh fruit and applesauce.

We looked at each other and asked, "What should we do?"

Three groups of people asked the same question of Jesus when He taught about the importance of producing good fruit—fruit that shows changed hearts and lives. Jesus told them that if a tree doesn't produce good fruit, it would be chopped down and tossed into the fire. It wasn't an outrageous pronouncement. That's what my husband seriously considered doing with our row of unproductive apple trees.

The people listening to Jesus asked, "What should we do?"

"And he answered them, 'Whoever has two tunics is to share with him who has none, and whoever has food is to do likewise'" (Luke 3:11). Jesus expected good fruit and generosity to follow.

"Tax collectors also came to be baptized and said to him, 'Teacher, what shall we do?' And he said to them, 'Collect no more than you are authorized to do'" (vv. 12 and 13). Jesus expected fairness and integrity.

"Soldiers also asked him, 'And we, what shall we do?' And he said to them, 'Do not extort money from anyone by threats or by false accusation, and be content with your wages'" (v. 14). Jesus said that a sign of good fruit is to be content with our pay.

Specific and practical advice. If we expect something loftier, we miss what good fruit looks like.

CYNTHIA RUCHTI

FAITH STEP

If a piece of fruit is part of your nutrition plan today, pause a moment before eating it and consider the fruit of your life.

TUESDAY
OCTOBER 29

"Give us this day our daily bread."

MATTHEW 6:11

SOMETIMES THINGS LOOM UP BEFORE us that seem impossible. Facing a big surgery, or the death of a loved one, or a lost job, or even a pile of unending laundry can feel like facing Mount Everest. We know that with God all things are possible, and we know He gives us the grace we need. But will it be enough? Fear closes in. Weakness. Uncertainty. How will we ever have enough strength to handle it?

I was thinking about this one day when I was baking bread. It smelled so good coming out of the oven. The dark gold color of the outside signaled perfect crispness. Like my Granny used to do, I rubbed butter over it, allowing it to melt into the fluffy interior. Before the bread could even cool, my family devoured a whole loaf.

This was fun, but it's not typical of our bread-eating behavior. We buy most of our bread at the store, and it comes pre-sliced. On Monday I use two slices for my husband's sandwich, and on Tuesday he gets two more. It's the same for my kids. Two slices each, slathered in peanut butter and jelly. Then two slices the next day. Not the whole loaf at once.

Our bread-eating habits are the perfect metaphor for how God's grace works—and His strength, His mercy, His power. When we're contemplating Mount Everest we may want the whole loaf, but God knows what is good for us. He knows what we really need. He slices off enough for the first step. Then, when it's time for the next one, another slice is there. And another and another and another till the journey is done. The whole loaf is ours—but God gives it as needed. Never too little, always just the right amount to fit our need.

GWEN FORD FAULKENBERRY

FAITH STEP

What is your deepest need today? Trust Jesus for it. He is Your manna from heaven.

WEDNESDAY
OCTOBER 30

*"It is God who arms me with strength and keeps
my way secure. He makes my feet like the feet of
a deer; he causes me to stand on the heights."*

2 SAMUEL 22:33–34 (NIV)

MY SUV ROUNDED THE CURVE and climbed farther
uphill. A moment later I saw the deer and instinctively braked.

We stared at each other briefly before he leaped effortlessly up the steep hillside. After making sure no vehicle was behind me, I gazed at the graceful animal as he joined two others waiting at the top.

I marveled at how perfectly God had fit the deer to move easily in their environment. Although deer begin life on trembling legs, Jesus strengthens and fine-tunes their muscles to handle rocky, hilly terrain with majestic grace.

Jesus works similarly in us by giving us the power we need to make it in the challenges of our environment. According to 2 Corinthians 1:21 (NLT), "It is God who enables us, along with you, to stand firm for Christ." In the challenges of living well for Jesus, His power in us gives us what we need to stand...and to stand *firm*. That concept is echoed in 1 John 2:13–14 (MSG): "Your fellowship with God enables you to gain a victory over the Evil One."

Jesus's vision for you is a victorious one. Just as deer wear the dignity and grace of their Creator, so do you. With Him, you can say, "Christ gives me the strength to face anything" (Philippians 4:13, CEV).

Whatever the heights of your challenges, Jesus desires to tone your spiritual muscles to handle them. Stand firmly on the truth that His strength empowers you.

ERIN KEELEY MARSHALL

FAITH STEP

What are you facing that needs a fresh vision of Jesus helping you to stand firmly in His power? Ask Him to give you what you need for your current environment.

THURSDAY
OCTOBER 31

Jesus asked, "Didn't I heal ten men?
Where are the other nine?"

LUKE 17:17 (NLT)

I TREASURE MY GRANDKIDS' RESPONSE to my little tokens of love for them. Freshly baked cinnamon buns or chocolate chip pancakes garner big hugs and sticky kisses. A bottle of bubbles or a package of stickers generates giant smiles and giggles. And always—no matter what the gift is—they say thank you.

Their parents have trained them to express gratitude, and as their grandmother, I've grown accustomed to them doing so. You could say I expect it from them. If they forget, I give them a gentle reminder: "Aren't you forgetting something?"

"Oh yeah," they say. "Thank you!"

Jesus expects us to thank Him too. We learn this from the story of the ten lepers. When only one leper expressed gratitude for restored health, Jesus appeared surprised. "The other nine—where are they?" He asked.

In the nine's defense, they'd run off to do what Jesus had told them to do—present themselves to the priest so he could declare them clean according to Old Testament law (Luke 17:14). He hadn't told them to say thank you first, had He? Why then was Jesus surprised when the nine ran away without expressing gratitude? Because He expected them to say thanks without needing a reminder.

Jesus lavishes tokens of His love on us every day. Forgiveness, peace, comfort, joy. These gifts and countless more warrant our gratitude. Let's remember to say thank You. He treasures our response.

GRACE FOX

FAITH STEP

Name three evidences of Christ's love for you. Take a moment to thank Him for these gifts.

NOVEMBER

FRIDAY
NOVEMBER 1

Jesus answered: "Watch out that no one deceives you. For many will come in my name, claiming, 'I am the Messiah,' and will deceive many."

MATTHEW 24:4–5 (NIV)

L AST WEEKEND, MY HUSBAND AND I hiked a small section of the Superior Hiking Trail in northern Minnesota. It was late autumn, so the maple forests had already shed their leaves, which added a new challenge to our hike. The underbrush had died, and the surrounding land was coated with the same carpet of leaves, so everything looked like a path.

When we live in a culture where so many claim to have answers for us, it can be difficult to discern the true path. The deceptions come not only from false religions or obvious cult leaders who claim to be a messiah. Many systems of thought can "come in His name," claiming to be compatible with the way of Jesus, even when they are not. Pursuing material wealth, chasing fame, elevating human wisdom as god—all are common temptations, even within our own churches.

Just as the volunteers who maintain the trail system have provided signs to guide us, Jesus has provided us with His Word in Scripture, so we can test each message we hear. He's also placed us within His body, the church, so we can practice discernment in community. He also nudges us in the right direction through His indwelling Holy Spirit.

Because of these gifts, we can journey without fear. Psalm 16:11 tells us, "You make known to me the path of life; you will fill me with joy in your presence, with eternal pleasures at your right hand" (NIV). As we seek His guidance, Jesus will steer us away from deceit and pitfalls. He will lead us forward on the path of serving Him with our lives.

SHARON HINCK

FAITH STEP

Take a walk or hike and thank Jesus for how He guides you away from dangers in your journey through life.

SATURDAY
NOVEMBER 2

No more dragging your feet! Clear the path for
long-distance runners so no one will trip and fall,
so no one will step in a hole and sprain an ankle.
Help each other out. And run for it!

HEBREWS 12:12–13 (MSG)

INEVITABLY, AS I WATCH the wrap-ups from various marathon races around our country each year, I see participants stumbling along with little chance of winning—maybe not even finishing. Yet news clips always zero in on the sidelines too, where well-wishers hoot and salute the runners on their journey. Occasionally, someone will even rush to a runner and physically help him or her across the finish line.

As I watch these scenarios unfold, I root for the underdogs, cheering them on, even offering a silent prayer that they will finish strong. And then the race is over.

Recently in Hebrews, I read about a race called life that is continual and one in which spectators offer encouragement before—and after—the runners cross the finish line. Only in this race, we are all participants. So how can we help others who may be lagging?

Confident that many have already finished successfully, we can cheer on others by slowing down and running beside them, prodding them to victory. We can pray for them and warn them of any pitfalls and problems we've already encountered. We can help them "run with perseverance" and visualize the goal—Jesus—waiting at the end. And we can encourage them often with words that say, "I care!" "Jesus is with you!" "You can do it!"

No one runs alone. The great thing about life is that all of us can not only finish but win—because of the One who ran before us, and along with us, all the way.

REBECCA BARLOW JORDAN

FAITH STEP

Review Hebrews 12 and list all of the ways you find to encourage both yourself and others toward life's finish line.

SUNDAY
NOVEMBER 3

"Give, and it will be given to you. A good measure, pressed down, shaken together and running over, will be poured into your lap. For with the measure you use, it will be measured to you."

LUKE 6:38 (NIV)

M Y HUSBAND, J.R., AND I travel often due to his business. When visiting other cities, we like to try different restaurants, places that aren't available in our home town. On a recent trip to New Orleans, we located a unique restaurant in the revived warehouse district.

What made the experience special wasn't the fabulous filet mignon, though it was delicious. It wasn't the Crawfish Monica, also amazing. And it wasn't even the banana cream pie that the owner brought out even though we didn't order the item (as he did with the sautéed carrots, creamed spinach and buttered potatoes). The experience was unique because there were no menus, no prices. The owner tells customers everything he has available, you tell him what you want and then he asks you to simply, "Pay what it's worth when you leave."

What a concept. We dined on one of the best meals I've had in years and we paid the owner generously for the experience. In fact, we paid even more because of his trust and generosity. The owner gave freely, and in turn received abundantly.

RENEE ANDREWS

FAITH STEP

Find a way today to give without expectation. Whether you receive abundantly in this life or in your eternal life, Christ has promised your cup will overflow. How glorious is that?

MONDAY
NOVEMBER 4

*"Dear brothers and sisters, when troubles of any
kind come your way, consider it an opportunity
for great joy. For you know that when your faith is
tested, your endurance has a chance to grow."*

JAMES 1:2–3 (NLT)

LAST NIGHT I WAS READING an article that focused on
being grateful for the difficulties of life. The hard places.
The struggles. The disappointments. They offer an opportunity for change, for overcoming, for a shift in worldview.

A Pulitzer–prize winning author who had been diagnosed
with melanoma took the diagnosis as a sign to pour his life
into helping others with melanoma by organizing runs for
research. I read that and thought, "Huh."

Because mostly, I am thankful for the things in my life
that are good, easy, and uplifting. The hard things? Not
so much.

But the author says that the struggles are like the contrast
in a painting that shows off the good in our lives. We can say,

"This time was incredibly difficult. But I made it through. And look at the beauty that can still be found in my life." We may not welcome troubles but we can welcome what Jesus can do with them.

Here are a few hard things I am grateful for: the experience of having a broken heart . . . because it showed me how amazing real love is. The rejections that I got for my fiction children's books . . . which started me on the path of writing adult nonfiction. The downward spiral I fell into in my college years . . . it sent me running back into the grace-filled arms of Jesus. But mostly, I am grateful for the rock-solidness of Jesus and the love of the people He has given me. I could have never gotten through the hard things without them.

SUSANNA FOTH AUGHTMON

FAITH STEP

Write your own hard gratitude list. Thank Jesus for what He has taught you in the midst of your struggles.

TUESDAY
NOVEMBER 5

Get rid of all bitterness, rage and anger, brawling and slander, along with every form of malice. Be kind and compassionate to one another, forgiving each other, just as in Christ, God forgave you.

EPHESIANS 4:31–32 (NIV)

A FEW NIGHTS AGO I went to bed with a prickly storm cloud in my heart. The week had been full of disappointments. I faced closed doors in my work that slammed with unnecessary harshness. Then when I'd approached friends for help they told me bluntly that they were too busy. Ongoing health challenges were flaring. As a distraction for the pain, I curled up to watch a movie, but the television wasn't working. From large hurts to petty frustrations, I felt like I was in the midst of brawling with the world.

The next morning, my husband brewed a pot of tea in our tea maker before he left for work. Much later, I poured a cup and took a sip. The tea tasted harsh and bitter. The pot had been sitting on the hot plate too long.

The taste reminded me of my grumpy mood. My hurts and disappointments had been simmering, growing more and more bitter. Time to dump out the old and start over.

"Lord, it's been a rough week. You know each thing that has caused me pain. But I need to stop simmering. I need to stop reviewing all the things that wounded me. Please forgive me for giving in to frustration when things didn't go my way. Wash me clean and start fresh."

I heated water for a new cup of tea and spent some time thanking God for His gifts—for times when friends had reached out and supported me, for work projects that had succeeded beyond my hopes, and for the comforts of my heating pad, quilt, and a warm house. Fresh tea washed away the aftertaste of bitterness, and gratitude replaced my bitter mood.

SHARON HINCK

FAITH STEP

Are there any injustices, disappointments, or frustrations that are on a low simmer in your heart? Ask Jesus to deal with them before they produce bitterness.

WEDNESDAY
NOVEMBER 6

*"When the Son of Man comes, will he
find faith on earth?"*

LUKE 18:8 (ESV)

FAMILIAR WITH MIDWESTERN SIGNS OF winter's approach, I perked up when a TV show mentioned the Alaskan version. In Alaska, when fireweed blossoms reach the top of their stalks, residents know to count on only 6 short weeks until winter. The plant is a beautiful sign of summer when it starts to bloom and a warning about winter's approach. If it blooms early, Alaskans hurry to stock up on firewood, fuel, and food for the long winter.

Hearty Alaskans know the value of careful preparation for winter. Those caught unaware will pay a heavy price.

Jesus gives us few details about His return. No fireweed blossoms. No save-the-date for our calendars. But He does tell us what He hopes and expects to find when He does return: faith. Fearless, relentless faith like that of the woman in Luke 18. Jesus used the persistent widow's prayer in a parable to teach us to "pray continuously and not to be discouraged."

We won't be caught unaware or unprepared for the moment of His return if we live faithful and faith-filled, day in and day out. If He comes on a Sabbath morning, He may find many of us in church, singing praises, giving, listening to God's Word. What if He comes on a random Wednesday afternoon? What then? Will He find faith at work?

To guarantee preparedness, we must let faith hem and define us 24-7. Jesus did not teach Sunday morning faith, but persistent, consistent, relentless faith that can't be caught unaware.

CYNTHIA RUCHTI

FAITH STEP

Think of one thing that might have to change so that no matter what hour of the day, what day of the week, or what year, when Christ returns, He'll find you living faithfully. What can you do today to transform that one into none?

THURSDAY
NOVEMBER 7

*"The thief's purpose is to steal, kill and destroy.
My purpose is to give life in all its fullness."*

JOHN 10:10 (TLB)

THE OTHER DAY I FOUND my four-year-old daughter, Stella, on the floor in front of her closet in a cluster of shoes. She'd try one on and toss it when it didn't meet her qualifications.

"Might I ask what on earth are you doing?"

"I'm finding the right shoes."

"Just pick some! It's time to go!"

"Mommy, I need to find the best pair for skipping!"

I can honestly say this was a new one. One Sunday after church she flung off her shoes as soon as we walked in the door and told me to throw them away because they were like tigers. When I gave her a puzzled look she explained how they bite and claw her feet. Needless to say, those shoes are no more. But skipping shoes?

My shoe philosophy is a lot more practical. I wear whatever matches, or what is most comfortable. Occasionally I'm fashion minded, pairing just the right boots with an outfit, or a dress with heels. But I've never really considered what shoes are best for skipping.

The thing is, we were going to the grocery store. There were no plans for skipping per se, but Stella's choice of shoes reflects her general outlook on the day. She didn't know and couldn't control what else was on the schedule. But she was planning on skipping.

I want my outlook to be more like that—to reflect more trust in Jesus when He says, "I came to give life... in all its fullness." John 10:10 (NCV). If His purpose for me is abundance, I need to plan on joy, no matter what the day brings.

GWEN FORD FAULKENBERRY

FAITH STEP

Make a to-do list for your day. Regardless of what's on it, don your skipping shoes before you step out, trusting that His plan for you is good.

FRIDAY
NOVEMBER 8

We know how troubles can develop passionate patience in us, . . . keeping us alert for whatever God will do next. In alert expectancy such as this, we're never left feeling shortchanged. Quite the contrary—we can't round up enough containers to hold everything God generously pours into our lives through the Holy Spirit!

ROMANS 5:3–5 (MSG)

"IF HE ASKS YOU TO put something down, it's because He wants you to pick up something greater." Someone recently posted that quote on Facebook. It's the promise of a better trade-off coming for those who feel shortchanged by something they feel Jesus is asking them to let go of in this life.

Read today's verses again in light of that hope.

I think a major reason for our culture's crazed drive to acquire is because of the underlying terror of knowing we will lose everything earthly at the end of this life. Without the eternal hope of Jesus to anchor us, we go nuts to think that we could lose all that is most precious here.

However, from Jesus's perspective, life on earth is about loss and letting go. From the first sin in Eden, we have been unable to save this world. Along with sin comes more loss. Even when we do our best for Him, we still are vulnerable to sin's effects.

Sometimes in living for Jesus, He asks us to let go of something we care for deeply so that He can do a greater work. Sometimes He allows terrible things because those things are part of this failing world. However, He promises to "repay you for the years the locusts have eaten" (Joel 2:25, NIV).

Jesus knows eternity with Himself and our heavenly Father will far, far, far surpass all that we lost on earth. In fact, it will wipe away all those losses and disappointments.

That hope doesn't completely remove our pain today, but it offers a glimpse into glory that we need to keep going.

ERIN KEELEY MARSHALL

FAITH STEP

What (or whom) have you lost in this life?
What hope does God offer for eternity that lifts
your heart in the here and now?

SATURDAY
NOVEMBER 9

Jesus also said, "The Kingdom of God is like a farmer who scatters seed on the ground. Night and day, while he's asleep or awake, the seed sprouts and grows, but he does not understand how it happens. The earth produces the crops on its own. First a leaf blade pushes through, then the heads of wheat are formed, and finally the grain ripens."

MARK 4:26–28 (NLT)

LAST WEEK I FELT AS if I accomplished nothing. Interruptions and distractions kept me from my plans. Like a farmer who has scattered seed and keeps peering at the field for a sign of life, I felt disheartened. What difference had I made for God's kingdom?

On the same day that I berated myself on my lack of harvest, a friend shared that she had been encouraged by my email to her. A reader wrote that one of my books had made a difference for her. My husband reminded me how often I make him laugh. It was as if Jesus was telling me that He is at work even when I am not seeing the results. In His parable in Mark, He shows us that the crops are growing even as the farmer sleeps. In fact, even though the farmer participates by planting seeds, the earth "produces the crops on its own."

Our job isn't to see how the crops are doing. Jesus invites us to generously plant our seeds of faith, and trust Him to bring the growth. He seems to accomplish most when we keep our focus on Him, not results. I like to imagine that in Heaven, Jesus will open a scrapbook and show us the marvelous things He was doing behind the scenes when we felt like our lives were barren fields. I still ask Him for glimpses now, because I find it so encouraging, but I'm gradually learning that I can trust that He is producing something of value in my life even when I can't see it.

SHARON HINCK

FAITH STEP

Think about the most empty field in your life.
Tell Jesus that you trust Him to produce
a harvest there and thank Him for that.

SUNDAY
NOVEMBER 10

*As long as the earth remains, there will be
planting and harvest, cold and heat,
summer and winter, day and night.*

GENESIS 8:22 (NLT)

LAST YEAR, MY HUSBAND AND I adopted two young
children from the foster care system. When they came
to us they'd already lived in five homes in six months. They
were anxious, and they had large emotional swings. I started
reading books to learn how to help them. We also visited
a trauma therapist. An important first step was to establish
a routine. For two children who didn't trust that they'd be
living in the same place tomorrow, a routine gave them sta-
bility. They flourished as they became grounded in wake-up
time, playtime, mealtimes, schooltime, and bedtime. When
they asked me what would be happening that day—and
I told them—I saw peace softening their little faces.

Sometimes we take for granted the peace that a routine
brings. From creation, God set up earth in a natural pattern.

"It was you who set all the boundaries of the earth; you made both summer and winter" (Psalm 74:17, NIV).

Winter may be hard, but we know spring is coming. Summer may be hot, but we anticipate autumn's cool breezes. In Genesis, Noah lived through a long year that included torrential rain, destruction, floating endlessly, and discovering a new landscape outside the ark window. As he emerged, God promised him the seasons and schedule would return.

Are you facing a hard time in life? Has darkness descended, or maybe the pressure is building and you're not sure if you can face the intensity much longer? Look outside your window, and remember that Jesus, too, works in seasons. What you face won't last forever. Jesus sets boundaries on the earth, and in your life.

TRICIA GOYER

FAITH STEP

Get out your camera, step outside, and snap a few photos of the season that you're in. As you do, pray and thank Jesus for the seasons in your life and faith walk.

MONDAY
NOVEMBER 11

*In every thing give thanks: for this is the will
of God in Christ Jesus concerning you.*

1 THESSALONIANS 5:18 (KJV)

NOVEMBER IS NOT MY FAVORITE month. It starts to get dark early, and I hate the dark. I also hate the cold. Both of these things make me want to stay in my pajamas all day and cuddle on the couch with my dog, but I must face my life. I have four human beings who depend on me to be sane and kind and responsible and wise. I feel my inadequacy in this child-rearing area every moment of every day. I see my time with them slipping through my fingers, and I get scared it won't be enough—I won't teach them enough or give them all they need to navigate life.

Like my kids, my parents are getting older, which I also hate. I don't see or talk to my friends enough and I miss them. My skin is awful. I've gained weight. Then there are my students and my job. And I won't even go into finances—always a fun topic this time of year.

People on social media have started the annoying practice again of posting things they are thankful for each day. *Even though I love Thanksgiving, I'm in no mood for thankful thoughts.* Thus went my grumpy inner dialogue on the way to work today, till I remembered Jesus and the fact that I really am thankful He loves me no matter what.

It seems that one glimmer of thankfulness opened the door to more things I am thankful for. I started to compose a mental list. And guess what? My grumpy anxiety gave way to peace, which was followed by joy.

GWEN FORD FAULKENBERRY

FAITH STEP

Grab a pen and paper and start writing down things you are thankful for, in no particular order. Don't stop till you feel His peace flowing like a river in your soul.

TUESDAY
NOVEMBER 12

I remind you to fan into flame the gift of God....

2 TIMOTHY 1:6 (ESV)

THERE IS NOTHING BETTER IN late fall than a crackling
fire in the woodstove. I love to curl up in a chair near it
with a good book or snuggle my family close while we gaze
at the dancing flames. Its light mesmerizes me.

Midway through this morning I hear the woodstove's fan
kicking in every couple of minutes as it tries to make the
most of the fading heat. I take a break from my work to
stoke the embers and add wood. Within minutes new flames
lick at the bark, and, soon after that, the fire climbs and
curls inside the firebox.

I head back to my office, and when the fan is satisfied I
hear it shut off. The house settles back into the warmth, and
I think about 2 Timothy 1:6—how we are to approach our
faith in Jesus with similar care.

Faith in God is a gift from Him, possible through Jesus's
life and death. But we play a role in its growth. If we don't

nurture our relationship with Jesus, its intensity eventually peters out.

However, when we feed it, it not only warms us from the inside; it spreads that warmth to everyone we are near. When we spend time each day feeding the fire of faith by reading God's Word and talking with Jesus, He does the supernatural work of stoking the flames.

When we ask Him to light the fire in us, Jesus can take the smallest spark of faith and set it ablaze. When we continue going to Him daily, we do our part to keep that fire burning in our hearts to warm the lives of a world in need of His light.

ERIN KEELEY MARSHALL

FAITH STEP

Read 2 Timothy 1 and ask Jesus to put it on your heart each day to care for the gift of faith He gives you.

WEDNESDAY
NOVEMBER 13

"I am the vine; you are the branches. If you remain in me and I in you, you will bear much fruit; apart from me you can do nothing."

JOHN 15:5 (NIV)

MY FRIEND JOYCE AND I play Scrabble over the Internet. She usually trounces me. Not only does she find creative words and ways to reach key double and triple word scores, she also remembers to play her words in ways that keep me from being able to access those spots. Perhaps her most effective skill, though, is her ability to find ways to let her word cozy up alongside another long word in play, creating not only her main word, but also a series of two-letter words that add up to a great score.

When Jesus talks about remaining in Him, I think about lining up alongside Him like those Scrabble words. My independent efforts are paltry at best. But when they are linked in to His grace, His purposes, His direction—connected as many places as possible—suddenly each activity and relationship can produce unexpected fruit. Bonus blessings, like the bonus points in Scrabble.

Once a Scrabble game has begun, a player can't place a random word off by itself on the board. Each word has to connect to another. In the same way, my life comes into play and my choices have meaning only when they intersect with what Jesus is doing.

SHARON HINCK

FAITH STEP

Pick one challenge in your life. Ask Jesus to show you how He is working out His purposes in that situation and ask Him to help you line up alongside Him.

THURSDAY
NOVEMBER 14

*"He cuts off every branch in me that bears
no fruit, while every branch that does bear fruit
he prunes so that it will be even more fruitful."*

JOHN 15:2 (NIV)

I'M LEARNING TO GROW GRAPES. I pictured myself harvesting and preserving grapes, but, for some reason, I never imagined myself pruning the vines. Then, the other day, when lasting snow was predicted, I walked the lane, clearing downed limbs and branches left from the Upper Peninsula's gales of November. There were a lot of them. Many trees had even fallen before the strength of the storms.

It occurred to me as I walked and pruned that God tends the forest like a vinedresser, but He uses mighty winds instead of hands. Old, brittle branches tumble to the forest floor. What's left is stronger, more ready for the weight of winter and buds of spring. God's winds ruthlessly thin the forest, leaving openings for new growth where an unbroken canopy would have prevented it.

I walked past my little vineyard and realized I hadn't been ruthless enough when the choices were up to me. In the above biblical quote, Jesus says *all* the unproductive branches had to go. That even the best branches had to be cut back to help them bear all the good fruit they were meant to make. But when I stood in the vineyard holding my pruning shears, I thought, *Really? This much? That can't be right*, and hesitated, afraid I'd kill the plants with all that cutting. In holding back, I didn't do the vines any favors. What seemed ruthless was more right than I could understand.

I'm glad the One who tends my life knows what's best for me, no matter how intense the pruning feels.

SUZANNE DAVENPORT TIETJEN

FAITH STEP

Are you going through some difficulty? Losing something or someone? Ask Jesus to help you to be more receptive to whatever (yes, whatever) He is doing in your life.

FRIDAY
NOVEMBER 15

I have given them the glory that you gave me,
that they may be one as we are one—I in them
and you in me—so that they may be
brought to complete unity.

JOHN 17:22–23 (NIV)

I LOVE TO MAKE "KITCHEN SINK" soup. It's made from
whatever veggies I find in the refrigerator and some
chicken broth. Two things are true about it: it's always
delicious, and it never comes out the same.

My world as a believer is like that pot of soup. Most of
the time I'm scrambling from one errand to another, and
I don't always know what Jesus has planned for me. Just as
unexpected ingredients meld together into a delicious meal,
I can be surprised at the "who" and "what" He adds into my
day. When peace and joy flood those unscheduled moments,
I stand in awe of His grace.

My faith life isn't made up solely of church and Bible
studies. Though those activities add flavor to my time just as

veggies build a tasty broth, they alone don't define me as a Christian. Instead, my trust in Jesus grows stronger as I meet the challenges He's chosen for me.

Jesus is with me every minute, helping me add spice to the lives of others. He knows what ingredients are missing, both in theirs and mine. As I reach out in obedience, He nourishes my soul.

HEIDI GAUL

FAITH STEP

Volunteer to serve at a soup kitchen, keeping watch for what and who Jesus adds into your time there. Notice how He feeds your faith as you act in obedience to Him.

SATURDAY
NOVEMBER 16

Leaving Nazareth, he went and lived in Capernaum, which was by the lake in the area of Zebulun and Naphtali—to fulfill what was said through the prophet Isaiah: "Land of Zebulun and land of Naphtali, the Way of the Sea, beyond the Jordan, Galilee of the Gentiles— the people living in darkness have seen a great light; on those living in the land of the shadow of death a light has dawned."

MATTHEW 4:13–16 (NIV)

IT HAS BEEN RAINING LIKE crazy. The sky is gray and murky with clouds. There is a general sense of wanting to huddle inside and drink cups of cocoa followed up by a lengthy nap.

We are Californians. We are used to sunshine. If the sun disappears we are at a loss. When it gets rainy, we go underground.

Sometimes my life feels rainy. And dark. No matter how many cups of cocoa I drink, I can't get free of that dark feeling. I told my cousin Beth just the other day, "When life is hard, I withdraw. I go off by myself and it's hard to find my way back." Darkness does that. It isolates. It creates shadows and fear and loneliness. But there is a light that pierces the dark. Two thousand years ago, Jesus did a number on the darkness, bringing to pass a prophecy that had been held at bay for hundreds of years. *People living in darkness had seen a great light. On those living in the land of the shadow of death a light has dawned.*

Beth and I talked about that too. On our darkest days is when we need Jesus most. His truth. His love. His grace. The Bright and Morning Star cracking the darkness with His fine and wondrous glory. And He still shines.

SUSANNA FOTH AUGHTMON

FAITH STEP

Sit in the sun while you take time to pray.
Soak up its warmth reminding you that
Jesus is the light in your darkness.

SUNDAY
NOVEMBER 17

"Hallelujah! Praise God from heaven, praise him from the mountaintops; Praise him, all you his angels, praise him, all you his warriors, Praise him, sun and moon, praise him, you morning stars; Praise him, high heaven, praise him, heavenly rain clouds; Praise, oh let them praise the name of God—he spoke the word, and there they were!"

PSALM 148:1–5 (MSG)

A CHILD'S PRAYERS HAVE TO be some of the sweetest words ever spoken.

In recent months my two-year-old daughter Calianne has begun to add her prayers at mealtimes and bedtime. Just as her dad and I have enjoyed listening to her older brother talk to God, we love the privilege of witnessing her communicate with her friend Jesus.

Two reasons I love her prayers are 1) they come straight from her heart—whatever is topmost in her thoughts, and 2) they're all about giving thanks. She's typically eager to pray, and she usually says something like this:

"Tanks you, Jesus, for pink fire trucks and for Daddy and Mama and Paxton-boy. And tanks you, Jesus, for doggies and yogurt and mine cozy bed. Amen—Go get it!"

I adore the "Go get it!" she adds to the end. We have no idea where she heard it; she said it came from her head. Knowing her, it probably did. Anyway, because her prayers are loaded with thanksgiving instead of requests, the "Go get it!" isn't a demand that Jesus do her beckoning. It's more like she's cheering Him on and praising Him: "You go, Jesus! You're the best!"

My children inspire me to be simple before Jesus, to praise Him with my first thoughts, to cheer Him on for being *Him*—for being my victorious Savior, attentive Friend, holy Lord and mighty King.

The unhindered, childlike approach to faith that Jesus spoke of in Luke 18:16–17 shows itself in how we communicate with Him. Let's bless Him with prayers of trust-filled praise. Go get it!

ERIN KEELEY MARSHALL

FAITH STEP

What typically characterizes your prayers? Praise? Requests? Complaints? Thanksgiving? Desperation? Trust? Offer it all to Him, paying special attention to praise and give thanks.

MONDAY
NOVEMBER 18

For I resolved to know nothing while I was with
you except Jesus Christ and him crucified.

1 CORINTHIANS 2:2 (NIV)

A S RECENT EMPTY NESTERS, MY husband and I have
begun thinking about downsizing. It's amazing how
much we've accumulated over the years. Sweaters seem
to reproduce in the back of the closet. Papers bulge in file
folders. Bins of outgrown toys fill the basement. As we sort
through things to donate or sell, we have an opportunity to
think about which items are really precious or needed, and
which things are simply clutter.

One of the challenges of sorting out clutter is that I rarely
have to make a simple choice between something good and
bad. Instead, there are lots of good things—just too many
of them.

Working at decluttering my home, I thought about the
rooms of my heart. I've also picked up some spiritual clutter
along my way. I've been excited by a particular trend in

worship or embraced a specific spiritual discipline or grappled with differing theological understandings of certain questions. But every now and then, Jesus reminds me to bring my focus back to what is absolutely essential—the simple core truth of His death and Resurrection.

I heard a story once that a leader of the Christian faith, with a wealth of intellect and scholarship at his disposal, was asked to summarize his beliefs. He chose to describe the central truth of the Gospel free from embellishment, in the words of the children's song, "Jesus loves me, this I know."

When I quiet all my opinions, knowledge and experiences, and everything else falls away, I can focus on that simple core truth, and rejoice.

SHARON HINCK

FAITH STEP

Are there any good things in your life getting in the way of the One best thing? Invite Jesus to clear away the clutter.

TUESDAY
NOVEMBER 19

*So then, just as you received Christ Jesus as
Lord, continue to live your lives in him, rooted and
built up in him, strengthened in the faith as you
were taught, and overflowing with thankfulness.*

COLOSSIANS 2:6–7 (NIV)

I FELT LIKE CRYING EVERY time I looked out my kitchen
window. Just a few weeks earlier, our maple trees had
been covered with golden leaves that glowed in the morning
sun. Now the leaves had fallen, and the stark, bare branches
showed the severe damage from an ice storm four years earlier. Heavy ice had accumulated on the trees that February,
eventually snapping off about a third of the top branches.
Seeing the broken tops of the trees made me feel hurt.

At least the maples still stood, lifting their branches
toward heaven as if in praise to their Creator. As I thought
about how deep and strong the trees' roots must be to with-
stand winds and winter ice storms, I remembered reading an
article about a giant redwood tree in California. Despite its

huge size, the tree had been knocked over by wind. The article explained that although giant redwoods can reach heights of more than 300 feet, they have shallow root systems. That got me thinking about my own "root system."

Jesus doesn't want His followers to stop at receiving Him as Savior and Lord. He wants us to sink our roots down deep into Him so we can grow up spiritually strong and healthy. I can help my faith develop deeper roots by nurturing my relationship with Jesus through Bible study, prayer, and obedience to His commands, service, and fellowship with other believers.

If my root system is shallow, I'll be in danger of being knocked down by the slightest winds of adversity or suffering. But when my roots go down deep into Christ, He will help me grow up straight and tall. I can lift my "branches" to Him in praise and thanks, no matter how storm-damaged they are.

DIANNE NEAL MATTHEWS

FAITH STEP

What are you doing to help your roots sink down deeper in Jesus and His Word?

WEDNESDAY
NOVEMBER 20

Humble yourselves, therefore, under God's mighty hand, that he may lift you up in due time. Cast all your anxiety on him because he cares for you.

1 PETER 5:6–7 (NIV)

OUR DOG, FLASH, IS A cross between a Jack Russell terrier and a Chihuahua. He is cute and fast and loves to play. He loves it when you throw him the ball. He just has one problem. Once he brings the ball back to you, he won't let it go. You can tell he wants to give it to you as he nudges it toward you. But as soon as you try and pick it up, he snatches it and growls. Then he looks at you, as if to say, "Why aren't you playing with me?"

The dog has issues. So do I. That is probably why I like him so much. I am just like Flash, who worries over his toy, constantly moving it around, never taking his eyes off it. This is what I do with my problems. I cannot let them go. I keep thinking about them, feeling sick to my stomach. All the while, my eyes are on Jesus and I am saying, "Why aren't

You doing anything about this? I keep bringing it to You." I bring my problem to Him. But I forget to let it go. I forget to say, "I would like You to take care of this, so I am placing it in Your hands."

When we pray, we are "tossing the ball." Laying our worries, our cares, our dreams at the feet of Jesus. But it is only when we have emptied our hearts and minds of our worries that He can fill us up with His overwhelming peace that passes all understanding.

SUSANNA FOTH AUGHTMON

FAITH STEP

Picture yourself throwing your "ball" of worries into the sky. Release them to Jesus's care and ask Him to fill you with His overwhelming peace.

THURSDAY
NOVEMBER 21

*For it is by grace you have been saved, through
faith—and this is not from yourselves, it is
the gift of God—not by works, so that no
one can boast. For we are God's handiwork,
created in Christ Jesus to do good works, which
God prepared in advance for us to do.*

EPHESIANS 2:8–10 (NIV)

OUR THREE-YEAR-OLD GRANDDAUGHTER LOVES TO help
in the kitchen, so her parents gave her a child-friendly
knife and cutting board. When my husband and I were
visiting and making a batch of chili, her mommy got out
her daughter's tools so she could sit at the table with me.
My husband cored a bell pepper and spread it out for her.
While I chopped onions, our granddaughter carefully diced
up the pepper. Later she helped me rinse the beans and add
them to the slow cooker.

That night at supper, she was delighted when we told her
daddy that she had helped make the chili. She couldn't read

a recipe, buy the produce, brown the ground beef, or create a meal all by herself. Her parents provided the tools and raw ingredients. My husband prepared the pepper. I supervised each moment and guided her. But she felt the joy of participating.

In the same way, Jesus gives us a gift that we could never create by our own efforts: salvation. He prepares good works for us to do. He guides us to the place where we can serve and empowers us each step of the way. We are as dependent as a three-year-old in the kitchen. There's no room for boasting in any step along the way. But there is plenty of room for joy. At the end of our lives we can—with the same joy as a little child—tell our heavenly Father, "I helped."

SHARON HINCK

FAITH STEP

Think about a good work that Jesus has led you to do.
Thank Him for preparing the task in advance
and empowering you each step of the way.

FRIDAY
NOVEMBER 22

Do not be anxious about anything,
but in everything by prayer and
supplication with thanksgiving let your
requests be made known to God.

PHILIPPIANS 4:6 (ESV)

OLD TESTAMENT AND NEW BOTH reinforce the notion
that gratitude is an important part of faith. Several times
in the Bible there appears to be a link between thankfulness
and prayer and admonitions against fretting. Why is that?

One explanation I hear orbits around first thanking God
for what we have before asking for something else. If we're
not grateful for what God has already provided, how can we
be grateful for His provision for what we now say we want
or need?

Some argue that it's more about affirming our grateful
confidence that God is hearing and will answer our prayers
than merely saying "thanks" for anything. Because, after
all, it's about trust. And while trusting God is a good thing,

in its extreme form, this belief can be a "name it, claim it" gimmick that makes God a genie rather than Sovereign of the Universe.

Personally, I've found the power of gratitude lies in changing my behavior. I can't manufacture the *feeling* of gratitude myself, but simply choosing to honor God by recognizing all that I have serves to frame my experience of His provision. Thanking God for everything also frees me from the fear that is so often about an unknown future; things I'm worried will or won't happen, things I will or won't get. When I approach His throne with an attitude of gratitude, I don't have to be anxious about anything.

ISABELLA CAMPOLATTARO

FAITH STEP

Identify a sister in Christ with whom you can share a daily Gratitude List via email or text. Start with three items, and work your way up.

SATURDAY
NOVEMBER 23

The Lord directs the steps of the godly.
He delights in every detail of their lives.

PSALM 37:23 (NLT)

IT WAS LATE NOVEMBER, AND I was flying from British Columbia to Saskatchewan to speak at two church events the next day. The first leg of my trip ended with a two-hour layover in Alberta. Unfortunately, a sudden blizzard canceled seven flights during that time—mine included. My first thought was *This can't be happening. What if the storm continues through the night? I'll miss my 9:00 AM event.*

The choice was mine. I could let the "what if" stress me, or I could believe that Jesus directs my steps and delights in every detail of my life—blizzards included. I chose the latter.

I will trust and not be afraid. Work out the details as You wish, I prayed silently as I joined the mile-long line at the ticket counter.

Jesus answered in an unexpected way. He immediately planted me beside a chatty young woman who spoke about her recent divorce, her new beau, and her desire for a loving, permanent marriage. Our conversation led to the importance of honoring one's spouse and what that looks like in day-to-day life. "This is all new to me," she said. "I'm really glad we met. I'm sure this was no accident."

My new friend and I parted ways two hours later. The blizzard lifted, and I caught a flight that enabled me to speak at my early-morning event.

Does Jesus orchestrate the details of our lives? Absolutely. And because He's loving and wise—and sees a bigger picture than we see—we don't need to fear or worry when He's in control.

GRACE FOX

FAITH STEP

Ask a friend to tell you about a time when Jesus clearly directed her circumstances. How did this grow her faith? Ask Jesus to give you opportunities to see Him obviously work on your behalf.

SUNDAY
NOVEMBER 24

All of us! Nothing between us and God, our faces shining with the brightness of his face. And so we are transfigured much like the Messiah, our lives gradually becoming brighter and more beautiful as God enters our lives and we become like him.

2 CORINTHIANS 3:18 (MSG)

THIS MORNING I SPENT MORE time than usual watching the fire in my little woodstove. I love to watch fires. I didn't have enough kindling so it took a little longer to get it started. Burning paper helped the cold chimney draw, and fat lighter wood eased the transition to the smallest available pieces of wood.

The fire caught with, first, a hiss and a wisp of smoke, and then finally a flicker of flame. It took more tending than usual so I spent some of that time on my belly, feet up behind me, my head on my hands like a kid.

Finally hot, the logs at the bottom maintained their form but gradually changed color. They abandoned their browns and began to glow, undulating orange. The color rippled like northern lights, occasionally allowing a glimpse of red or yellow.

Fine gray ash coated the logs, but the light shone through. Each finally reached a point where it wasn't what it had been before. The log shapes had become nearly weightless containers for heat and light. When I put dry, cold wood near them, the heat set the new pieces ablaze.

When I was finally forced to make room for more wood, I hated to reach for the poker. The oldest of the coals dissolved into ash with the slightest touch, while newer ones broke into pieces, still carrying their treasure, ready to pass it on.

We transition too. Because Christ is in us, we can't stay the same. Daily, with our assent, we are changed into His likeness.

SUZANNE DAVENPORT TIETJEN

FAITH STEP

Old paintings of Jesus sometimes show His burning heart. See your heart aflame like His. Let Him change you.

MONDAY
NOVEMBER 25

Let your conversation be always full of grace,
seasoned with salt, so that you may
know how to answer everyone.

COLOSSIANS 4:6 (NIV)

IT'S JUST DAYS BEFORE THANKSGIVING, and the country is aflutter with reminders to be grateful. From social-media updates to morning-show news features to devotions like these, we are reminded to give thanks.

These are great words to recall as we cook and clean and prepare. I've got my shopping list ready and my spice rack at attention as I consider the dishes I'm adding to the menu.

And I'm also reminded that being watchful with our words of gratitude should be part of everyday life. It isn't just the holidays when we can be stretched to find the right response to a stressful family member or when our patience is taxed by words that grate on us. And it isn't only a handful of special days when responsibilities, disappointments, difficult memories, and battles with character growth wear on us.

During this season of Thanksgiving, it's worthwhile to start and stop our conversations with the words of Colossians 4:6. Grace filled Jesus's talk no matter if He was affirming someone's faith or calling a person out on sin. Grace doesn't brush over the truth when it needs to shine in the darkness. Neither does it withhold forgiveness or mercy when those are called for.

Offering grace is like seasoning just the right amount, which is always appropriate to make the recipe delectable. Grace is appetizing; everyone's got a taste for it, and we all hunger for it. Let's follow Jesus into the day and season our conversation with His grace, trusting that His Spirit will guide us to the right response at the right time.

ERIN KEELEY MARSHALL

FAITH STEP

Think of a time when you did not offer a response Jesus would have offered. Now think of a time when you did. Ask Him to flavor your conversation.

TUESDAY
NOVEMBER 26

I have been crucified with Christ, and it is no longer I who live, but it is Christ who lives in me. And the life I now live in the flesh I live by the faith of the Son of God, who loved me and gave himself for me.

GALATIANS 2:19–20 (NRSVUE)

SOMETIMES IT SEEMS WHAT WE do is so little. I feel it when I am folding clothes, washing dishes, tying my baby's shoes, doing homework with my six-year-old, and packing my husband's lunch. I feel it when I pray for my eleven-year-old on his spelling test, when I send my teenager a text of encouragement before her game. I feel it when I play the piano for a church of seventy-five members and teach a class of twenty-five students.

The hope for all of these things is in the story of the little boy with his loaves and fishes. He offered what he had. Not much. But Jesus took his small offering and increased it. He does the same with us.

John writes, "Unless a grain of wheat falls into the ground and dies, it remains alone; but if it dies, it produces much grain" (12:24, NKJV). We may feel as if we're constantly falling short, but even Jesus seemed to fall short at the Cross. All of His efforts met with apparent defeat. Yet three days later He rose from the grave.

The greatest theme of the story of Jesus is this—redemption. Life out of death. When we are "crucified with Christ," putting self to death, we are also raised with Him, to walk in newness of life. It is Jesus Who lives His life in us and through us. This turns all of our "little things" into things that matter, deeds with divine purpose, seeds that fall to the ground only to produce a harvest beyond our wildest dreams.

GWEN FORD FAULKENBERRY

FAITH STEP

Lord Jesus, help us to remember that everything
Your spirit ordains for us to do, no matter how
small it may seem, is of great value in the kingdom
of heaven. Help us to work for You today.

WEDNESDAY
NOVEMBER 27

Then he took the seven loaves and the fish, and
when he had given thanks, he broke them and gave
them to the disciples, and they in turn to the people.

MATTHEW 15:36 (NIV)

ALL THE BURNERS ON MY stove were busy with potatoes, gravy, and green beans. The oven wafted scents
of roasting turkey. As we prepared for family to arrive
for Thanksgiving dinner, music played from my iPod. I
hummed along as I stirred the gravy. "I love my Thanksgiving mix," I said to my husband. "All of my favorite hymns
and great praise music. I always look forward to listening to it
on the holiday."

My husband checked the turkey. "You know, you could
play it on other days."

I laughed. "I know, but I never think of it."

It struck me then; his reminder applied to more than
music. I whispered a prayer, "Lord, help me turn on a
thanksgiving mix in my heart each and every day."

Jesus gave a consistent example of gratitude during His time on earth. Scripture records several instances where He gives thanks. In Matthew's account, He demonstrates a thankful heart for the miracle God was about to supply—before it even unfolded.

We don't have to wait until prayers are answered the way we wish before we express gratitude. We don't have to wait for special occasions and holidays. Like Jesus, we can give thanks during our everyday living and during the anticipation of blessings to come. Let's set the music of our soul on a selection of appreciation, contentment, and joy and hear it play all day long.

SHARON HINCK

FAITH STEP

Play a favorite Thanksgiving hymn.
Watch for opportunities to give thanks
at various moments throughout your day.

THANKSGIVING DAY
THURSDAY
NOVEMBER 28

*Return to your home, and recount [the story] of how
many and great things God has done for you. And
[the man] departed, proclaiming throughout the
whole city how much Jesus had done for him.*

LUKE 8:39 (AMPC)

I REMEMBER GOING TO MY grandparents' mobile home for
Thanksgiving dinner as a child. I'd sit at the kids' table
with my brother and two cousins. I was the oldest, and it
was work trying to keep my younger cousins out of trouble.
I'd eat until my belly was full, and while my brother and
cousins played outside I'd listen to the grown-ups talk. I was
interested in their world, their stories.

Now I'm the grown-up. I'm the one in the kitchen cook-
ing. I'm also the one sitting with the other adults sharing
stories. Each family has important stories that need to be
passed on and shared. We often talk about how my grand-
father grew up in Kansas and moved to California during

the Dust Bowl. Or about how my grandmother was born to Mexican immigrants and grew up in a boxcar. John and I even share funny stories like how our first VCR had a remote control that was connected to the box by a long cord. Or the first time I saw someone with a car phone (before cell phones). But most of all we love sharing stories about our faith—about answered prayers and the ways Jesus has shown up. It's these stories that pass down a heritage of faith.

It's important to go out and to share the good news of Jesus with others, but it's also important to start at home. Thanksgiving is a time for family, and it's a time for sharing stories. Family members know our strengths and weaknesses, high and lows. They can also see Jesus's transformation in our lives, and then desire it for their own.

TRICIA GOYER

FAITH STEP

Think of one personal faith story to share at your Thanksgiving celebration, and pray for the perfect moment to share it.

FRIDAY
NOVEMBER 29

God is the one who uncovers what
lies deeply hidden; he knows what
hides in darkness; light lives with him!

DANIEL 2:22 (CEB)

A WINDSTORM LATE IN THE fall stripped the last of the
leaves clinging to their branches, with the thick woods
near our home left exposed. Where in midsummer we could
see only a few feet into the woods because of the leaves
and underbrush, with the underbrush bare and the trees
denuded, our line of sight extended hundreds of feet farther.

What we saw were all of the tripping hazards that had
been hidden when the woods were lush with growth. Half-
downed trees. Stumps. The litter from those who had used
the road nearby. The hazards became much easier to see,
identify, and clear away with the leaves gone.

Are there tripping hazards in your life that are hidden
when all is at its peak, calm and untroubled? When the wind
blows cold and hard, or you enter a dry, bitter, seemingly

lifeless season, does the lack of growth uncover those problem areas?

Jesus carries a big chain saw and knows how to use a chipper/shredder. He loves it when we invite Him to clear away the debris—those downed trees, those resentments and past hurts and ungodly affections that can pose a hazard. Rather than shy away from that cleanup task when the wind is howling and you can't see a sign of life, let Him use that time to His and to your advantage.

CYNTHIA RUCHTI

FAITH STEP

There's a sweet intimacy in letting Jesus have access to the debris-strewn parts of our lives, the areas not yet yielded to Him. Don't fear the process. Embrace it.

SATURDAY
NOVEMBER 30

*One of them, when he saw that he was
healed, came back to Jesus, shouting, "Praise
God!" He fell to the ground at Jesus' feet,
thanking him for what he had done.*

LUKE 17:15–16 (NLT)

WHILE DRIVING TO A CONFERENCE many years ago,
an old childhood fear resurfaced. I already felt a bit
nervous since I wasn't used to traveling alone, especially
along an unfamiliar route. But my hands clenched the
steering wheel when I suddenly found myself on a very old
and extremely narrow bridge. Each side consisted of a single,
rusty metal rail. To make matters worse, the bridge arced
upward over the river. "Help me Lord help me Lord help me
Lord...," I repeated out loud all the way across. When my
wheels hit the level pavement again, I relaxed and breathed.
"Thank You, Lord!"

Some time passed before I realized that while I probably
repeated the prayer for help ten times in those few moments,

I only said one thank-you after I crossed the bridge. One out of ten—similar to the numbers when Jesus healed a group of ten lepers. The dreaded, debilitating and disfiguring disease had made these men outcasts from society, but Jesus gave them a fresh start in life. Yet only one of them returned to thank his healer. Jesus wondered aloud where the other nine were.

I'm sure there are times when Jesus wonders where my gratitude is. How can I forget to give thanks to the One Who forgave my past, died to secure my future and fills my present life with blessings? Expressing thankfulness to Jesus not only pleases Him but helps me grow in my understanding of Him. A grateful spirit also prepares my heart to receive more blessings from Him, which gives me more reason to thank Him. And gratitude is a wonderful cycle to be caught in.

DIANNE NEAL MATTHEWS

FAITH STEP

Can you think of any blessings or answers to prayer that you have taken for granted? Be like the one leper and remember to thank Jesus for what He has done in your life.

Autumn and Thanksgiving 2024
Reflections and Memories

Autumn and Thanksgiving 2024
Reflections and Memories

Autumn and Thanksgiving 2024
Reflections and Memories

Autumn and Thanksgiving 2024
Reflections and Memories

CONTRIBUTORS

Renee Andrews: 30, 78

Susanna Foth Aughtmon: 34, 80, 104, 112

Isabella Campolattaro: 20, 32, 116

Gwen Ford Faulkenberry: 22, 52, 66, 86, 94, 124

Grace Fox: 16, 58, 70, 118

Heidi Gaul: 46, 102

Tricia Goyer: 56, 92, 128

Jeanette Hanscome: 40

Sharon Hinck: 18, 26, 36, 48, 60, 74, 82, 90, 98, 108, 114, 126

Rebecca Barlow Jordan: 54, 76

Erin Keeley Marshall: 10, 24, 38, 68, 88, 96, 106, 122

Dianne Neal Matthews: 12, 28, 62, 110, 132

Cynthia Ruchti: 14, 50, 64, 84, 130

Camy Tang: 44

Alice Thompson: 42

Suzanne Davenport Tietjen: 100, 120

A NOTE FROM THE EDITORS

We hope you enjoyed *Walking with Jesus: Devotions for Autumn and Thanksgiving 2024,* published by Guideposts. For over 75 years, Guideposts, a nonprofit organization, has been driven by a vision of a world filled with hope. We aspire to be the voice of a trusted friend, a friend who makes you feel more hopeful and connected.

By making a purchase from Guideposts, you join our community in touching millions of lives, inspiring them to believe that all things are possible through faith, hope, and prayer. Your continued support allows us to provide uplifting resources to those in need. Whether through our communities, websites, apps, or publications, we inspire our audiences, bring them together, and comfort, uplift, entertain, and guide them. Visit us at guideposts.org to learn more.

We would love to hear from you. Write us at Guideposts, P.O. Box 5815, Harlan, Iowa 51593 or call us at (800) 932-2145. Did you love *Walking with Jesus: Devotions for Autumn and Thanksgiving 2024*? Leave a review for this product on guideposts.org/shop. Your feedback helps others in our community find relevant products.

Find inspiration, find faith, find Guideposts.

Shop our best sellers and favorites at
guideposts.org/shop

Or scan the QR code to go directly to our Shop